Rethinking International Development series

Series Editors
Ray Kiely
Queen Mary University of London
London, UK

Andy Sumner
King's College London, UK

Rethinking International Development is dedicated to publishing cutting-edge titles that focus on the broad area of 'development'. The core aims of the series are to present critical work that is cross disciplinary, challenges orthodoxies, reconciles theoretical depth with empirical research, explores the frontiers of development studies in terms of 'development' in both North and South and global inter-connectedness, and reflects on claims to knowledge and intervening in other people's lives.

More information about this series at
http://www.palgrave.com/gp/series/14501

Lukas Schlogl · Andy Sumner

Disrupted Development and the Future of Inequality in the Age of Automation

Lukas Schlogl
University of Vienna
Vienna, Austria

Andy Sumner
King's College London
London, UK

Published with the support of the Austrian Science Fund (FWF): PUB 676-Z

Der Wissenschaftsfonds.

Rethinking International Development series
ISBN 978-3-030-30130-9   ISBN 978-3-030-30131-6 (eBook)
https://doi.org/10.1007/978-3-030-30131-6

© The Editor(s) (if applicable) and The Author(s) 2020, corrected publication 2020.
This book is an open access publication.

Open Access This book is licensed under the terms of the Creative Commons Attribution 4.0 International License (http://creativecommons.org/licenses/by/4.0/), which permits use, sharing, adaptation, distribution and reproduction in any medium or format, as long as you give appropriate credit to the original author(s) and the source, provide a link to the Creative Commons license and indicate if changes were made.

The images or other third party material in this book are included in the book's Creative Commons license, unless indicated otherwise in a credit line to the material. If material is not included in the book's Creative Commons license and your intended use is not permitted by statutory regulation or exceeds the permitted use, you will need to obtain permission directly from the copyright holder.

The use of general descriptive names, registered names, trademarks, service marks, etc. in this publication does not imply, even in the absence of a specific statement, that such names are exempt from the relevant protective laws and regulations and therefore free for general use.
The publisher, the authors and the editors are safe to assume that the advice and information in this book are believed to be true and accurate at the date of publication. Neither the publisher nor the authors or the editors give a warranty, expressed or implied, with respect to the material contained herein or for any errors or omissions that may have been made. The publisher remains neutral with regard to jurisdictional claims in published maps and institutional affiliations.

Cover credit: Cultura Creative (RF)/Alamy Stock Photo

This Palgrave Pivot imprint is published by the registered company Springer Nature Switzerland AG
The registered company address is: Gewerbestrasse 11, 6330 Cham, Switzerland

The original version of this book was inadvertently published without the acknowledgement of the funder (Austrian Science Fund (FWF): PUB 676-Z). The book has been updated with the changes. The correction to the book is available at https://doi.org/10.1007/978-3-030-30131-6_8

Acknowledgements

The authors are grateful for comments from Tony Addison, Artur Borkowski, Charles Kenny, Kyunghoon Kim, Joerg Mayer, Terry McKinley, Paul Segal, Dharendra Wardhana, Leslie Willcocks, Chunbing Xing and an anonymous reviewer, as well as participants at the Economic and Social Research Council (ESRC) Global Poverty & Inequality Dynamics Research Network workshop, March 27–28, 2018, London. All errors and omissions are our own. This book was produced as part of an ESRC Global Challenges Research Fund Strategic Research Network (Grant ES/P006299/1). The authors are grateful for receiving a grant from the Austrian Science Fund (FWF), which facilitated Open Access publication.

Contents

1 Introduction   1

Part I   The Contemporary Context for Economic Development in the Developing World

2 Economic Development and Structural Transformation   11

3 Deindustrialization and Tertiarization in the Developing World   21

Part II   The Future of Economic Development, Work and Wages in the Developing World

4 Technological Transformation   37

5 Automation and Structural Transformation in Developing Countries   51

6 Automation, Politics, and Public Policy   79

| 7 | Conclusions | 85 |

Correction to: Disrupted Development and the Future of Inequality in the Age of Automation — C1

References — 89

Index — 99

List of Figures

Fig. 3.1	GDP and employment shares by region, 1960–present	23
Fig. 3.2	Growth decomposition by sector, by region, 1960–present (change in growth = 100)	24
Fig. 3.3	Growth decomposition by factor, by region, 1970–present (change in growth = 100)	25
Fig. 3.4	Labor productivity versus GDP per capita, by region, 1960–present	26
Fig. 3.5	Composition of exports by regions, 1960–present	27
Fig. 3.6	Trade shares, 1961–present (or available years)	28
Fig. 5.1	Structural change in a "dual economy" defined by automatability	56
Fig. 5.2	The level of economic development and the share of employment susceptible to automation	66
Fig. 5.3	Employment by sectors and GNI per capita (2016 or most recent data)	68
Fig. 5.4	Automatability and share of employment by sectors, 2016	69
Fig. 5.5	McKinsey Global Institute's automatability estimates and employment across economic sectors by income group	70
Fig. 5.6	Economic development and sectoral employment shares across countries (fitted lines): 1991 and 2014	71

List of Tables

Table 4.1	Determinants of the feasibility of automation	40
Table 5.1	The labor dynamics of automation in a dual economy	62
Table 5.2	Estimates of the employment impact of automation	63
Table 5.3	Estimates of the proportion of employment that is automatable in selected countries	65
Table 6.1	The space of potential public policy responses to automation	81

CHAPTER 1

Introduction

Abstract Automation is likely to impact on developing countries in different ways to the way automation affects high-income countries. The poorer a country is, the more jobs it has that are in principle automatable because the kinds of jobs common in developing countries—such as routine work—are substantially more susceptible to automation than the jobs that dominate high-income economies. This matters because employment generation is crucial to spreading the benefits of economic growth broadly and to reducing global poverty. We argue that the rise of a global "robot reserve army" has profound effects on labor markets and structural transformation in developing countries, but rather than causing mass unemployment, AI and robots are more likely to lead to stagnant wages and premature deindustrialization. As agricultural and manufacturing jobs are automated, workers will continue to flood the service sector. This will itself hinder poverty reduction and likely put upward pressure on national inequality, weakening the poverty-reducing power of growth, and potentially placing the existing social contract under strain. How developing countries should respond in terms of public policy is a crucial question, affecting not only middle-income developing countries, but even the very poorest countries.

Keywords Automation · Digitization · Labor-saving technology · Developing countries · Economic development · Jobs

© The Author(s) 2020
L. Schlogl and A. Sumner, *Disrupted Development and the Future of Inequality in the Age of Automation*, Rethinking International Development series, https://doi.org/10.1007/978-3-030-30131-6_1

1

1.1 Introduction

A specter is haunting the industrialized and developing world—the specter of automation. 1.8 bn jobs or two-thirds of the current labor force of developing countries are estimated to be susceptible to automation from *today's* technological standpoint, according to the World Bank (2016). Employment generation is crucial to spreading the benefits of economic growth broadly and to reducing global poverty. And yet, emerging economies face a contemporary challenge to traditional pathways to employment generation: automation, digitization, and labor-saving technologies.

A broad range of international agencies have recently flagged such issues relating to the future of employment, and the consequences of automation and deindustrialization in their global reports (ADB, 2018; Hallward-Driemeier & Nayyar, 2017; ILO, 2017; IMF, 2017; UNCTAD, 2017; UNDP, 2015; UNIDO, 2016; World Bank, 2013, 2016) and the International Labor Organization (ILO) has launched a Global Commission on the Future of Work. Employment prospects have also come into sharp focus because of the contested experiences of "premature deindustrialization" (Palma, 2005; Rodrik, 2016) and weakening employment elasticities of growth.[1]

There is currently significant and rising interest in these issues in the scholarly community (see e.g. Acemoglu & Restrepo, 2017; Arntz, Gregory, & Zierahn, 2016; Grace, Salvatier, Dafoe, Zhang, & Evans, 2017; Mishel & Bivens, 2017; Mokyr, Vickers, & Ziebarth, 2015; Roine & Waldenström, 2014), in the reports of international agencies (see references above), and in the private sector too (Frey, Osborne, & Holmes, 2016; McKinsey Global Institute, 2017a, 2017b; PWC, 2017; World Economic Forum, 2017). Moreover, the topic has also captured the public interest, reflected by a mushrooming of media reports and popular science books on the issues (e.g. Avent, 2017; Brynjolfsson & McAfee, 2011, 2014; Harari, 2016; Srnicek, 2017, to name but a few). Despite this increasing interest, the effects of automation in particular remain highly contestable and understudied with respect to developing economies, given that most research has focused on high-income Organisation for Economic Co-operation and Development (OECD) countries such as the United States.

These are, however, not only OECD country issues (see discussion of Ahmed, 2017). The World Bank (2016, pp. 22f.) estimates that "the share of occupations that could experience significant automation is actually higher in developing countries than in more advanced ones, where many of these jobs have already disappeared." However, they note that the impact will be moderated by wage growth and the speed of technology adoption. There are numerous estimates of job displacement and much in the way of gray literature. However, these estimates are based on contestable assumptions and analysis of developing countries is often limited.

Furthermore, in contrast to a widespread narrative of technological unemployment, a more likely impact in the short-to-medium term at least is slow real-wage growth in low- and medium-skilled jobs as workers face competition from automation. This will itself hinder poverty reduction and likely put upward pressure on national inequality, weakening the poverty-reducing power of growth, and potentially placing the existing social contract under strain, or even possibly limiting the emergence of more inclusive social contracts. How developing countries should respond in terms of public policy is a crucial question, affecting not only middle-income developing countries, but even the very poorest countries given the automation trends in agriculture.

1.2 The Contribution and Structure of This Book

In light of the above, the objective of this book is to do the following: First, to outline a set of schools on economic development and revisit the Lewis model of economic development; second, to sketch the contemporary context of deindustrialization and tertiarization in the developing world; third, to survey the literature on automation; and in doing so discuss definitions and determinants of automation in the context of theories of economic development and assess the empirical estimates of employment-related impacts of automation; fourth, to characterize the potential public policy responses to automation and fifth, to highlight areas for further research in terms of employment and economic development strategies in developing countries.

The book is structured as follows. We set the scene in Part I (Chapters 2 and 3). We discuss the context for contemporary economic development in the developing world. Specifically, Chapter 2 gives an overview of schools of economic development theory and revisits the Lewis model of economic development. Chapter 3 then outlines the contemporary context of deindustrialization and tertiarization in the developing world to set the scene.

In Part II we focus on the emergence of automation and the drivers, implications for economic development and issues for developing countries. Chapter 4 discusses the trends in technology and discusses definitions and determinants of automation. Chapter 5 discusses the effect of automation on economic development and employment in developing countries from a theoretical perspective. Further, it analyzes existing empirical forecasts of automatability and global patterns. Chapter 6 considers the public policy responses proposed. Finally, Chapter 7 concludes and highlights areas for further research in terms of employment and economic development strategies in developing countries.

Note

1. Heintz (2009) examines employment growth and the productivity growth rate in 35 countries between 1961 and 2008, and finds that increases in the productivity growth rate slow down the rate of employment growth, and that this pattern is getting stronger over time. In the 1960s, a one percentage point increase in the growth rate of productivity reduced employment growth by just 0.07 percentage points. However, in the 2000s, that same one percentage point increase in the growth rate of productivity reduced employment growth by a substantial 0.54 percentage point. Several possible explanations are as follows: (i) it could be that increases in productivity over time are reducing the employment elasticity of growth; (ii) it could be that the proportion of wage labor is increasing; or (iii) it could be that increases in real wages, employers' social contributions, or strengthening labor institutions are raising unit labor costs and dampening employment creation, though this is ambiguous in empirical studies. A meta-review of 150 studies of labor institutions (Betcherman, 2012) covering minimum wages, employment protection regulation, unions and collective bargaining, and mandated benefits) with an emphasis on studies in developing countries, found that in most cases, effects are either modest or work in both directions in terms of productivity.

References

Acemoglu, D., & Restrepo, P. (2017). *Robots and jobs: Evidence from US labor markets* (NBER Working Paper Series No. 23285). Cambridge, MA: NBER. Retrieved from http://www.nber.org/papers/w23285.

ADB (Asian Development Bank). (2018). *Asian development outlook 2018: How technology affects jobs*. Manila: ADB.

Ahmed, M. (2017). Technological revolution and the future of work. *Center for global development blog*. Retrieved May 25, 2018, from https://www.cgdev.org/blog/technological-revolution-and-future-work.

Arntz, M., Gregory, T., & Zierahn, U. (2016). The risk of automation for jobs in OECD countries: A comparative analysis. *OECD Social, Employment and Migration Working Papers, 2*(189), 47–54.

Avent, R. (2017). *The wealth of humans: Work and its absence in the twenty-first century*. London: Penguin Random House.

Betcherman, G. (2012). *Labor market institutions: A review of the literature* (World Bank Policy Research Working Paper Series No. 6276). Washington, DC: World Bank.

Brynjolfsson, E., & McAfee, A. (2011). *Race against the machine: How the digital revolution is accelerating innovation, driving productivity, and irreversibly transforming employment and the economy*. Lexington, MA: Digital Frontier Press.

Brynjolfsson, E., & McAfee, A. (2014). *The second machine age: Work, progress, and prosperity in a time of brilliant technologies*. New York, NY and London: W. W. Norton.

Frey, C. B., Osborne, M. A., & Holmes, C. (2016). *Technology at work v2.0: The future is not what it used to be* (Citi GPS: Global Perspectives & Solutions). Oxford. Retrieved from http://www.oxfordmartin.ox.ac.uk/downloads/reports/Citi_GPS_Technology_Work_2.pdf.

Grace, K., Salvatier, J., Dafoe, A., Zhang, B., & Evans, O. (2017). *When will AI exceed human performance? Evidence from AI experts* (arXiv No. 1705.08807v2). Retrieved from http://arxiv.org/abs/1705.08807.

Hallward-Driemeier, M., & Nayyar, G. (2017). *Trouble in the making? The future of manufacturing-led development*. Washington, DC: World Bank.

Harari, Y. N. (2016). *Homo deus: A brief history of tomorrow*. London: Harvill Secker.

Heintz, J. (2009). *Employment, economic development and poverty reduction: Critical issues and policy challenges*. Geneva: UNRISD.

ILO. (2017). *The future of work we want: A global dialogue*. Geneva: International Labor Organization. Retrieved from http://www.ilo.org/global/topics/future-of-work/WCMS_570282/lang–en/index.htm.

IMF. (2017). *World economic outlook, April 2017: Gaining momentum?* Washington, DC: IMF. Retrieved from http://www.imf.org/en/Publications/WEO/Issues/2017/04/04/world-economic-outlook-april-2017.

McKinsey Global Institute. (2017a). *A future that works: Automation, employment, and productivity*. Retrieved from https://www.mckinsey.com/~/media/McKinsey/Global%20Themes/Digital%20Disruption/Harnessing%20automation%20for%20a%20future%20that%20works/MGI-A-future-that-works_Full-report.ashx.

McKinsey Global Institute. (2017b). *Jobs lost, jobs gained: Workforce transitions in a time of automation*. Retrieved from https://www.mckinsey.com/~/media/McKinsey/Global%20Themes/Future%20of%20Organizations/What%20the%20future%20of%20work%20will%20mean%20for%20jobs%20skills%20and%20wages/MGI-Jobs-Lost-Jobs-Gained-Report-December-6-2017.ashx.

Mishel, L., & Bivens, J. (2017). *The zombie robot argument lurches on: There is no evidence that automation leads to joblessness or inequality*. Washington, DC: Economic Policy Institute. Retrieved from http://www.epi.org/files/pdf/126750.pdf.

Mokyr, J., Vickers, C., & Ziebarth, N. L. (2015). The history of technological anxiety and the future of economic growth: Is this time different? *Journal of Economic Perspectives, 29*(3), 31–50.

Palma, J. G. (2005). Four sources of "de-industrialization" and a new concept of the "Dutch disease". In J. A. Ocampo (Ed.), *Beyond reforms: Structural dynamic and macroeconomic vulnerability* (pp. 71–116). Palo Alto, CA and Washington, DC: Stanford University Press and World Bank.

PWC (PricewaterhouseCoopers). (2017). UK Economic Outlook.

Rodrik, D. (2016). Premature deindustrialization. *Journal of Economic Growth, 21*(1), 1–33.

Roine, J., & Waldenström, D. (2014). *Long-run trends in the distribution of income and wealth* (IZA Discussion Paper No. 8157). Bonn: IZA. Retrieved from ftp.iza.org/dp8157.pdf.

Srnicek, N. (2017). *Platform capitalism*. Cambridge and Malden, MA: Polity Press.

UNCTAD. (2017). *Trade and development report 2017—Beyond austerity: Towards a global new deal*. New York and Geneva: UNCTAD.

UNDP. (2015). *Work for human development: Human development report*. New York: UNDP.

UNIDO. (2016). *Industrial development report 2016: The role of technology and innovation in inclusive and sustainable industrial development*. Vienna: UNIDO.

World Bank. (2013). *World development report: Jobs*. Washington, DC: World Bank.

World Bank. (2016). *World development report: Digital dividends*. Washington, DC: World Bank.

World Economic Forum. (2017). *Impact of the fourth industrial revolution on supply chains*. Geneva: WEF.

Open Access This chapter is licensed under the terms of the Creative Commons Attribution 4.0 International License (http://creativecommons.org/licenses/by/4.0/), which permits use, sharing, adaptation, distribution and reproduction in any medium or format, as long as you give appropriate credit to the original author(s) and the source, provide a link to the Creative Commons license and indicate if changes were made.

The images or other third party material in this chapter are included in the chapter's Creative Commons license, unless indicated otherwise in a credit line to the material. If material is not included in the chapter's Creative Commons license and your intended use is not permitted by statutory regulation or exceeds the permitted use, you will need to obtain permission directly from the copyright holder.

PART I

The Contemporary Context for Economic Development in the Developing World

CHAPTER 2

Economic Development and Structural Transformation

Abstract Technological change affects the sectoral composition of an economy. But, (why) do economic sectors matter? We revisit three schools of theory on economic development: the "classical," the neo-Schumpeterian and the neoclassical school. While the latter two camps are agnostic toward the role of economic sectors in development, the first places a special emphasis on sectoral—particularly, manufacturing—development as an engine of growth. In the tradition of W. Arthur Lewis and Nicholas Kaldor among others, development is thus envisaged as "structural transformation" of production and employment. We show that the classical view, and its more recent iterations, continues to find empirical support in its lasting explanatory power.

Keywords Development theory · Structural transformation · Economic sectors · Neoclassical theory · Schumpeter · Lewis model

2.1 Three Schools of Economic Development Theory

Palma (2005) usefully outlines three schools broad schools of theory on economic development, in terms of how each views sector and activity specificity (and includes caveats for oversimplicity). There are two schools—neoclassical and neo-Schumpeterian—which are, in general, based on the assumption that an equilibrating process due to marginal returns leads to an optimal allocation of factors of production at least in the medium-to-long term. These schools see little importance in sectors although the latter is concerned with activities. In contrast, a third school—a Lewisian or Kaldorian or even simply, the classical school, given its historic roots—where sectors matter as does activity specificity. This is to the point that manufacturing is special as it has increasing returns to scale (in direct contrast to neoclassical theory of constant or decreasing returns to scale), provides a host of spillovers and there is a core premise that equilibrium may not prevail and a structural imbalance—in the sectoral distribution of factors of production—which is not optimal for economic development and growth may persist even in the long run.

The first school—neoclassical theory—is indifferent to sectors and specificity of economic activity (Herrendorf, Rogerson, & Valentinyi, 2014). This school is represented by Solow convergence models (traditional and augmented), endogenous models based on increasing returns, and models based on market imperfections in technological change. Although the importance of the shift to higher productivity is not disputed in neoclassical economics, a one-sector model of economic growth has become standard in macroeconomics. In this one-sector model of economic growth there is no account of the process of inter-sectoral reallocation of economic activity or structural transformation. This is because, in the neoclassical growth model (of Solow, 1956), growth is driven by incentives to save, accumulate physical and human capital, and innovate. The neoclassical position is that poor countries will grow faster than rich countries and countries with the same technology will converge at a similar income level (see discussion in Sutirtha, Kessler, and Subramanian, 2016). A second school—neo-Schumpeterian—like the neoclassical school, is indifferent to sectors too. However, this neo-Schumpeterian school is concerned with economic activities specificity. This school is associated with Roemer and the neo-Schumpeterians who argue that research and development matter, but that there is nothing special about manufacturing in terms of increasing returns to scale of manufacturing or positive spillovers for example.

The third school, which may be labeled as the Classical School given its roots in Ricardo and classical political economy or the Lewis-Kaldor School given the elucidation of economic development as structural transformation in both Lewis (see for example, 1954, 1958, 1969, 1972, 1976, 1979) and Kaldor (1957, 1967, 1978 [1966]) among others such as Chenery (1960, 1975, 1979), Hirschman (1958), Myrdal (1957a, 1957b, 1968), and Thirlwall (1982, 2011). What binds this group together is that growth dynamics are dependent on the activities being developed and the capital accumulation effects of manufacturing. Thus, issues such as technology, externalities, balance of payment sustainability, and convergence with advanced countries are a function of the size, strength, and depth of manufacturing.[1] Many such as Rodrik (2016) argue that most services are (i) non-tradable, and (ii) not technologically dynamic, and that (iii) some sectors are tradable and dynamic, but they do not have the capacity to absorb labor. Similar shortcomings can be observed about the manufacturing sector. A significant share of manufacturing is (i) non-traded (even though it is tradable), (ii) much of manufacturing in developing countries is not technologically advanced (at least in relative terms to other modern sectors), and (iii) where some manufacturing sectors are technologically dynamic, they may not create much employment, as some service sectors do.

Empirically, McMillan and Rodrik (2011, p. 1), in taking sectoral and aggregate labor productivity data empirically, show that the transfer of labor and other inputs to higher productive activity is a driver of economic development, as Lewis hypothesized. They go on to note that structural transformation (ST) can in fact be growth-enhancing or growth-reducing depending on the reallocation of labor. This is an important point and relates to the multiple modes of ST and direction between sectors, which may be regressive as well as progressive in the sense of productivity gains or losses. They show how structural change had been growth-enhancing in Asia because labor has transferred from low to higher productivity sectors. However, the converse is the case for sub-Saharan Africa and Latin America because labor has been transferred from higher to lower productivity sectors and this has reduced growth rates.[2]

McMillan and Rodrik (2011) find that countries with a large share of exports in natural resources tend to experience growth-reducing structural transformation and, even if they have higher productivity, cannot absorb surplus labor from agriculture. In a similar vein, Gollin, Jedwab, and Vollrath (2016), too, argued that natural resource exports drive urbanization without structural transformation because natural resources generate considerable surplus which is spent on urban goods and services, and urban employment tends to be in non-traded services. McMillan and Rodrik (2011) also find that an undervalued (competitive) exchange rate, which operates effectively as a subsidy on industry and labor market characteristics (so labor can move across sectors and firms easily), leads to growth-enhancing structural transformation. In a similar vein, Diao, McMillan, Rodrik, and Kennedy (2017) argue that the most recent growth accelerations in the developing world, unlike East Asia's historical experience, have not been driven by industrialization but by within-sector productivity growth (in Latin America) and growth-increasing structural transformation, but this has been accompanied by negative labor productivity growth within nonagricultural sectors (in Ethiopia, Malawi, Senegal, and Tanzania). Others, such as Herrendorf et al. (2014), concur empirically with the argument that the sectoral composition of economic activity is key to understanding not only economic development but also regional income convergence, productivity trends, business cycles, and inequality in wages.[3]

2.2 Economic Development with Structural Transformation: Kaldor Revisited

The theoretical basis or model of economic development of the third school, as noted, is that associated with Nicholas Kaldor and Arthur Lewis. The special characteristics of manufacturing argument is predicated on the work of Kaldor (1967). Kaldor posited that economic development requires industrialization because increasing returns in the manufacturing sector mean faster growth of manufacturing output which is associated with faster economic growth. Kaldor's arguments were because backward and forward input–output linkages are strongest in manufacturing, and the scope for capital accumulation, technological progress, economies of scale, and knowledge spillover are strong. Further, there is a strong causal relationship between manufacturing output growth and labor productivity because of a deepening division of labor, specialization, and learning-by-doing, and the scope for productivity gains is large due to economies of scale.

Kaldor (1978 [1966], 1967) outlined a set of empirical regularities which came to be known as "Kaldor's growth laws" that are framed around ST (see for discussion in particular Storm, 2015; Targetti, 2005).[4] Kaldor (1967) sought to explain the economic development of Western Europe through the development of manufacturing which he argued was the engine of growth for every country at every stage of economic development. He posited that: (i) Economic development requires industrialization because increasing returns in the manufacturing sector mean faster growth of manufacturing output which is associated with faster GDP growth. This is because backward and forward input–output linkages are strongest in manufacturing and the scope for capital accumulation, technological progress, economies of scale and knowledge spillover are strong. Further, there is a strong causal relationship between manufacturing output growth and labor productivity because of a deepening division of labor, specialization, and learning-by-doing and the scope for productivity gains is large due to economies of scale; (ii) industrialization requires a basis in agricultural modernization to ensure food supply and labor will transfer from other sectors to manufacturing. As manufacturing grows, productivity across the economy will rise even in agriculture and services through positive spillovers such as technological knowhow and complementary markets in services. Kaldor argued that the agriculture and industrial sectors are not only connected by the Lewis labor transition (the elastic supply of labor is due to industry wages exceeding agriculture wages) but also because agriculture creates autonomous demand for the manufacturing sector and thus land reform is required if agriculture is not to hinder ST; (iii) aggregate demand should be managed to ensure growth (e.g. policies on public investment, taxation, directed credit); and (iv) as exports become increasingly important as a source of demand for the manufacturing sector as the economy grows, global competition requires temporary domestic industry protection accompanied by export-led growth policies.[5] In sum, for Kaldor, the virtuous cycle or Myrdal's cycle of cumulative causation is that demand and output growth fuel productivity growth due to increasing returns to scale which in turn fuels capital accumulation.

It is Kaldor's second law, also known as Kaldor-Verdoorn law, that contains a tension of particular importance to ST and inclusive growth. The Kaldor-Verdoorn (respectively, 1966 and 1949) coefficient is the employment elasticity of growth. The more manufacturing grows the more productivity grows across the whole economy because manufacturing provides capital goods across the economy. This is because increases in manufacturing employment raise agriculture productivity (as labor migrates) and because the manufacturing sector is the only sector with static and dynamic returns to scale due to new processes.[6] Kaldor's (1978 [1966]) interpretation of Verdoorn (1949) is that output growth induces improvements in labor productivity (assuming an elastic labor supply) and not vice versa. In contrast, the hypothesis of neoclassical models such as Solow is that productivity growth is due to technological progress. Verdoorn's argument was one of cumulative causation where demand rather than supply determines the rate of accumulation. From this basis Kaldor (and later Thirlwall) developed models where the growth of exports leads to specialization which then leads to increases in productivity and skills improvements. This then causes resources to move to the export sector.[7]

2.3 Economic Development with Structural Transformation: Lewis Revisited

Arthur Lewis (see notably, 1954, 1958, 1969, 1972, 1976, 1979) provided one of the best-known models of economic development in developing countries. Although sixty years old in its earliest iteration, the model remains relevant today to developing countries (see for contemporary discussion, Gollin, 2014). The dual model provides a heuristic device or an ideal type, in the Weberian sense, for thinking about structural transformation and economic development with an emphasis on labor, which is the factor of production that dominates most developing countries.

Lewis argued that the driver of capital accumulation was a sectoral movement of labor, from the "traditional" or "subsistence" or "non-capitalist" sector (of low productivity, low wage, priced to average product not marginal product, and thus with widespread disguised unemployment) to the "modern" or "capitalist" sector (of higher productivity, and where wages are set by productivity in the "subsistence sector"). Crucial is the existence of surplus labor in the traditional or noncapitalist sector. Because of this wages are set just above subsistence across the whole economy, leading to the transfer of labor over time from traditional or noncapitalist to modern or capitalist sectors and the capture of labor productivity gains to capitalists as profits as these are the source of growth via reinvestment. The floor for wages is institutionally set at subsistence. When the surplus labor disappears an integrated labor market and economy emerge and wages will then start to rise.

The Lewis model was intended as a critique of the neoclassical approach in that labor is available to the modern or capitalist sector of an economy not in a perfectly elastic supply but upward sloping rather than flat, and with a distinction between surplus-producing labor and subsistence labor (the latter of which was a negligible source of net profits for reinvestment, which Lewis saw as the driver for growth). Lewis also rejected the assumptions of neoclassical economists of perfect competition, market clearing and full employment and Lewis (see 1958, pp. 8, 18) made the distinction between productive labor, which produced a surplus, and unproductive labor, which did not.

There have been various critiques of the Lewis model, many of which are of a "red herring" variety as Ranis (2004, p. 716) puts it, meaning they are easily responded to or actually criticisms of Lewisians rather than the writing of Lewis himself. Many relate to the assumption of labor abundance in the subsistence sector (and thus the dominance of the wage from that sector across the economy), and the emergence of the urban informal sector, although Lewis's conception of surplus labor explicitly included the urban informal sector (see discussion in Fei & Ranis, 1964; Harris & Todaro, 1970; Minami, 1973; Rosenzweig, 1988; Schultz, 1964; Todaro, 1969).

A set of contemporary challenges throws up greater levels of complexity. First, domestic labor migration may not be permanent but circular (back-and-forth) or "commuting." Second, the contemporary scale of inter-sectoral resource flows via the growth of remittances further blurs the line between sectors. Finally, the Lewis transition can take a variety of forms beyond the anticipated one by Lewis and it is by no means guaranteed that the transfer will be from low- to high-productivity activities as flagged by McMillan and Rodrik (2011). A transfer from low-productivity agriculture to low-productivity services has been the experience of many developing countries and a reversing of the Lewis transition has also been a phenomenon noted in a number of developing countries in "premature deindustrialization."

In sum, the Classical School approach to economic development is that economic development is driven by changing structures of GDP and employment that lead to productivity growth. As a result of the productivity rates between sectors differing so substantially, the transfer of labor and production is a major source of productivity gains and thus economic growth.

Notes

1. One hybrid is Diao et al. (2017, pp. 3–4) seek to link the structural dualism of Lewis with the neoclassical model by arguing that the neoclassical model shows the growth process within the modern sector and the dual model shows the relationship among sectors.

2. McMillan and Rodrik (2011) find that countries with a large share of exports in natural resources tend to experience growth-reducing structural transformation and, even if they have higher productivity, cannot absorb surplus labor from agriculture. In a similar vein, Gollin et al. (2016), too, argued that natural resource exports drive urbanization without structural transformation because natural resources generate considerable surplus which is spent on urban goods and services, and urban employment tends to be in non-traded services. McMillan and Rodrik (2011) also find that an undervalued (competitive) exchange rate, which operates effectively as a subsidy on industry and labor market characteristics (so labor can move across sectors and firms easily), leads to growth-enhancing structural transformation.
3. There are a set of methodological questions too. Syrquin (2007) briefly identifies such questions and they include defining what is meant by "sectors" and thus what ST means (inter- or intra-depends on the breadth of definitions of sectors) and the blurring between "services" and "manufacturing" due to technological advances and outsourcing.
4. Targetti (1988) highlights Kaldor's contribution in cumulative causation rather than timeless "equilibrium."
5. Kaldor also took the two-sector model to be applicable to trade between developing and developed countries through the export of agriculture products from the former and import of manufactured goods from the later. He argued that international trade could make developing countries poorer because liberalization would increase agriculture exports which are produced at decreasing returns that are not sufficient to compensate for the loss of manufacturing exports, which is a sector which produces increasing returns.
6. In contrast, the neoclassical position on growth and employment is based on Okun's (1962) law which states that changes in the GDP growth rate and rate of unemployment have a negative association. This was critiqued for not accounting for changes that could be due to alterations in labor force participation (see Basu & Foley, 2013).
7. Thirlwall (1979) added that the rate of economic growth will not exceed the rate of growth of exports to the income elasticity of demand for imports. In short, he argued that there is a balance of payments constraint on growth.

References

Basu, D., & Foley, D. K. (2013). Dynamics of output and employment in the US economy. *Cambridge Journal of Economics, 37*(5), 1077–1106.

Chenery, H. B. (1960). Patterns of industrial growth. *The American Economic Review, 50*(4), 624–654.

Chenery, H. B. (1975). The structuralist approach to development policy. *The American Economic Review, 65*(2), 310–316.

Chenery, H. B. (1979). *Structural change and development policy*. Washington, DC: World Bank and Oxford Oxford University Press.

Diao, X., McMillan, M., Rodrik, D., & Kennedy, J. F. (2017). *The recent growth boom in developing economies: A structural-change perspective* (NBER Working Paper Series No. 23132). Cambridge, MA: NBER. Retrieved from http://www.nber.org/papers/w23132.

Fei, J. C. H., & Ranis, G. (1964). *Development of the labor surplus economy: Theory and policy*. Homewood, IL: Richard A. Irwin.

Gollin, D. (2014). The Lewis model: A 60-year retrospective. *Journal of Economic Perspectives, 28*(3), 71–88.

Gollin, D., Jedwab, R., & Vollrath, D. (2016). Urbanization with and without structural transformation. *Journal of Economic Growth, 21*(1), 35–70.

Harris, J. R., & Todaro, M. P. (1970). Migration, unemployment and development: A two-sector analysis. *American Economic Review, 60*, 126–142.

Herrendorf, B., Rogerson, R., & Valentinyi, A. (2014). *Growth and structural transformation* (NBER Working Paper Series No. 18996). Cambridge, MA: NBER. Retrieved from http://www.nber.org/papers/w18996.

Hirschman, A. O. (1958). *The strategy of economic development*. New Haven, CT: Yale University Press.

Kaldor, N. (1957). A model of economic growth. *The Economic Journal, 67*(268), 591–624.

Kaldor, N. (1978 [1966]). *Causes of the slow rate of economic growth of the United Kingdom*. Cambridge: Cambridge University Press.

Lewis, W. A. (1954). Economic development with unlimited supplies of labour. *The Manchester School of Economic and Social Studies, 22*(2), 139–191.

Lewis, W. A. (1979). The dual economy revisited. *The Manchester School, 47*(3), 211–229.

McMillan, M. S., & Rodrik, D. (2011). *Globalization, structural change and productivity growth* (NBER Working Paper Series No. 17143). Cambridge, MA: NBER. Retrieved from http://www.nber.org/papers/w17143.

Minami, R. (1973). *The turning point in economic development: Japan's experience*. Tokyo: Kinokuniya.

Myrdal, G. (1957a). *Rich lands and poor: The road to world prosperity*. New York: Harper & Brothers.

Myrdal, G. (1957b). *Economic theory and underdeveloped regions*. London: Gerald Duckworth & Co. Ltd.

Myrdal, G. (1968). *Asian drama: An inquiry into the poverty of nations*. New York: Pantheon Books.

Palma, J. G. (2005). Four sources of "de-industrialization" and a new concept of the "Dutch disease". In J. A. Ocampo (Ed.), *Beyond reforms: Structural dynamic and macroeconomic vulnerability* (pp. 71–116). Palo Alto, CA and Washington, DC: Stanford University Press and World Bank.

Ranis, G. (2004). *'Arthur Lewis' contribution to development thinking and policy* (Discussion Paper 891). Economic Growth Center Yale University.

Rodrik, D. (2016). Premature deindustrialization. *Journal of Economic Growth, 21*(1), 1–33.
Rosenzweig, M. (1988). Labor markets in low income countries. In H. Chenery & T. N. Srinivasan (Eds.), *Handbook of development economics* (Vol. 1). Amsterdam: North Holland Press.
Solow, R. M. (1956). A contribution to the theory of economic growth. *The Quarterly Journal of Economics, 70*(1), 65–94.
Storm, S. (2015). Structural change. *Development and Change, 46,* 666–699.
Sutirtha, R., Kessler, M., & Subramanian, A. (2016). *Glimpsing the end of economic history? Unconditional convergence and the missing middle-income trap* (Centre for Global Development Working Paper 438). Washington, DC: CGD.
Syrquin, M. (2007). *Kuznets and Pasinetti on the study of structural transformation: Never the Twain shall meet?* (International Centre for Economic Research Working Paper 46). Torino, Italy.
Targetti, F. (1988). 'Nicholas Kaldor', *Teoria e politica economica di un capitalismo in mutamento.* Bologna: Società Editrice II Mulino S.p.A.
Targetti, F. (2005). Nicholas Kaldor: Key contributions to development economics. *Development and Change, 36*(6), 1185–1199.
Thirlwall, A. P. (1979). The interaction between income and expenditure in the absorption approach to the balance of payments. *Journal of Macroeconomics, Elsevier, 1*(2), 237–240.
Thirlwall, A. P. (1982). Deindustrialisation in the UK. *Lloyd's Bank Review, 134,* 22–37.
Thirlwall, A. P. (2011). Balance of payments constrained growth models: History and overview. *PSL Quarterly Review, 64*(259), 307–351.
Todaro, M. P. (1969). A model of labor migration and urban unemployment in less developed countries. *The American Economic Review, 59,* 138–148.

Open Access This chapter is licensed under the terms of the Creative Commons Attribution 4.0 International License (http://creativecommons.org/licenses/by/4.0/), which permits use, sharing, adaptation, distribution and reproduction in any medium or format, as long as you give appropriate credit to the original author(s) and the source, provide a link to the Creative Commons license and indicate if changes were made.

The images or other third party material in this chapter are included in the chapter's Creative Commons license, unless indicated otherwise in a credit line to the material. If material is not included in the chapter's Creative Commons license and your intended use is not permitted by statutory regulation or exceeds the permitted use, you will need to obtain permission directly from the copyright holder.

CHAPTER 3

Deindustrialization and Tertiarization in the Developing World

Abstract This chapter outlines the contours of contemporary structural change and economic development along the following lines: in all developing regions agriculture shares of GDP and employment have fallen substantially—albeit they still persist at high levels among the poorest countries; regional manufacturing shares are consistent with deindustrialization or stagnant industrialization in employment shares and value-added; and, service shares of GDP and employment are on an upward trend in general, with the exception of East Asian economic growth, which has been driven by an inter-sectoral movement toward manufacturing. There is also a trend toward greater capital intensity of growth. Further, while in East Asia there have been substantial changes in the composition of exports, this is not the case in all regions.

Keywords Deindustrialization · Tertiarization · Service sector · Growth decomposition · Labor productivity · Trade

3.1 A Sketch of Contemporary Economic Development and Structural Transformation

In this section, a sketch of the empirical experience of economic development and structural transformation (ST) in the developing world is discussed to set the later discussion in an empirical context. One could

© The Author(s) 2020
L. Schlogl and A. Sumner, *Disrupted Development and the Future of Inequality in the Age of Automation*, Rethinking International Development series, https://doi.org/10.1007/978-3-030-30131-6_3

say that a conceptualization of ST has three discernible dimensions framed around a shift toward higher productivity activities. These are sectoral, factoral, and integrative. The first dimension—the sectoral aspects of ST—is about the inter- and intra-reallocation of sectoral activity toward higher productivity. The second dimension is the factoral aspects of ST and is about the composition or drivers of economic growth in terms of a shift of factors of production toward higher productivity activities. Third are the integrative aspects of ST. This is the extent of integration in terms of the global economy and a shift from forms of incorporation—trade deficits and capital inflows that come with liabilities (for example, profit repatriation or debt repayment)—toward trade surpluses.

The Groningen Growth and Development Centre (GGDC) 10-Sector Database (version 2014) developed by Timmer, de Vries, and de Vries (2015) provides a long-run, comparable dataset on value-added, employment and exports for ten economic sectors covering thirty-three developing countries covering the period since the 1950s. The GGDC 10-Sector Database covers eleven countries in Africa; eleven in Asia; nine in Latin America; and two in the Middle East and North Africa. The GGDC 10-Sector Database can thus be used to consider ST over time in developing countries.[1]

Additionally, the specific limitations of the GGDC 10-Sector Database are discussed by Diao, McMillan, Rodrik, and Kennedy (2017, pp. 4–6) who note the following: (i) the data broadly include all employment regardless of formality or informality, but the extent to which the value-added data do so depends on the quality of national sources (see Timmer et al. 2015); (ii) the quality of data from poor countries and Africa in particular is questioned, though it is noted that Gollin (2014) have shown high correlations between national accounts data and sectoral measures of consumption which is reassuring, and the African countries in the GGDC dataset are those with the strongest national statistical offices; (iii) the measurement of labor inputs is not by hours but number of employees in a sector: thus seasonality might lead to an underestimation of labor productivity in agriculture for example, though it is noted that Duarte and Restuccia (2010) find a correlation between hours worked and employment shares in a set of twenty-nine developed and developing countries; and (iv) if labor shares differ greatly across economic activities, then comparing average labor productivity can be misleading.

We use the data here to give a broad brush of ST in the developing world since the 1960s and the identification—or proof of concept—of new modes of ST in terms of the identification of deindustrialization and tertiarization in some parts of the developing world since around 2000. Figures 3.1–3.6 illustrate ST in the developing world cover in turn, sectoral ST, factoral ST, and integrative ST.

First, sectoral ST: we are interested in the extent and trajectory of ST —in terms of sectoral allocations of GDP, and employment and exports. How one reacts to such graphs depends, in part, on assumptions made about privileging manufacturing in terms of productivity and

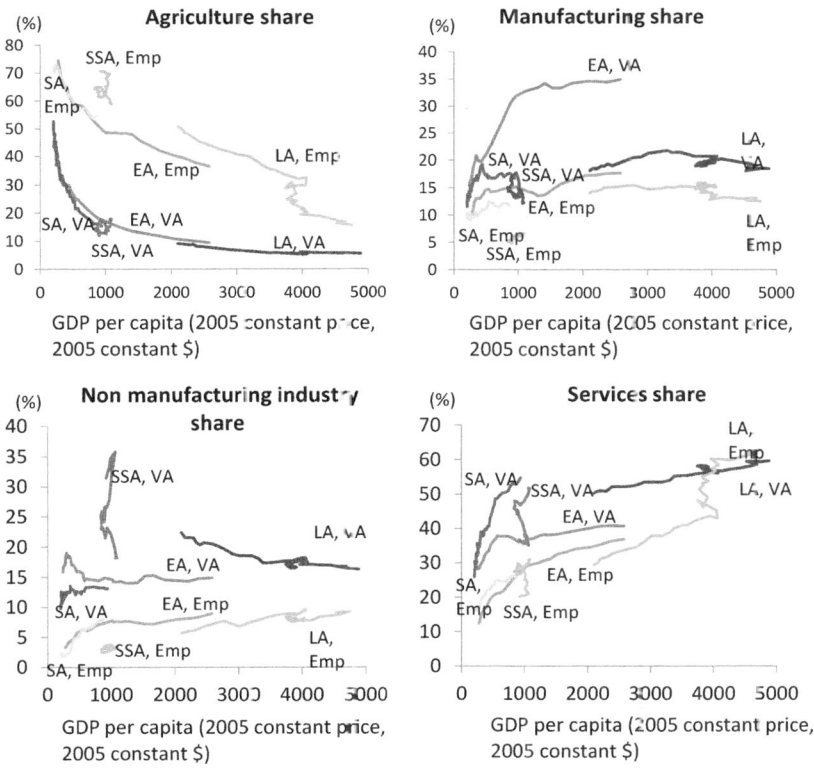

Fig. 3.1 GDP and employment shares by region, 1960–present. *Source* Author's calculation based on Timmer et al. [2015]

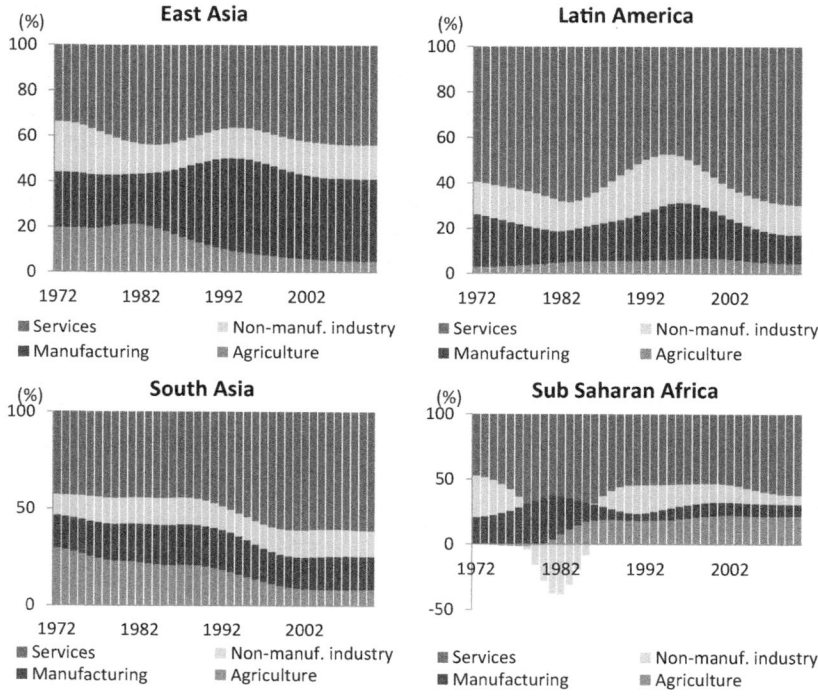

Fig. 3.2 Growth decomposition by sector, by region, 1960–present (change in growth = 100). *Source* Author's calculation based on Timmer et al. [2015]

employment generation potential vis-à-vis services (see later discussion). Figure 3.1 shows the sectoral structure of GDP and employment relative to GDP per capita (and one can also assess the relative labor or capital intensity of regional production by the position of the value-added and employment curves: if the employment curve is above the value-added curve then production in that sector and region is relatively more capital intensive).

As is well known, the agriculture component is falling in share of GDP and employment in all regions and is very low in Latin America. In East Asia, the declining shares of agriculture in GDP and employment over the period is notable relative to other regions. The rise in manufacturing shares in East Asia's GDP over the period is particularly impressive, though this is less the case for employment shares. This suggests

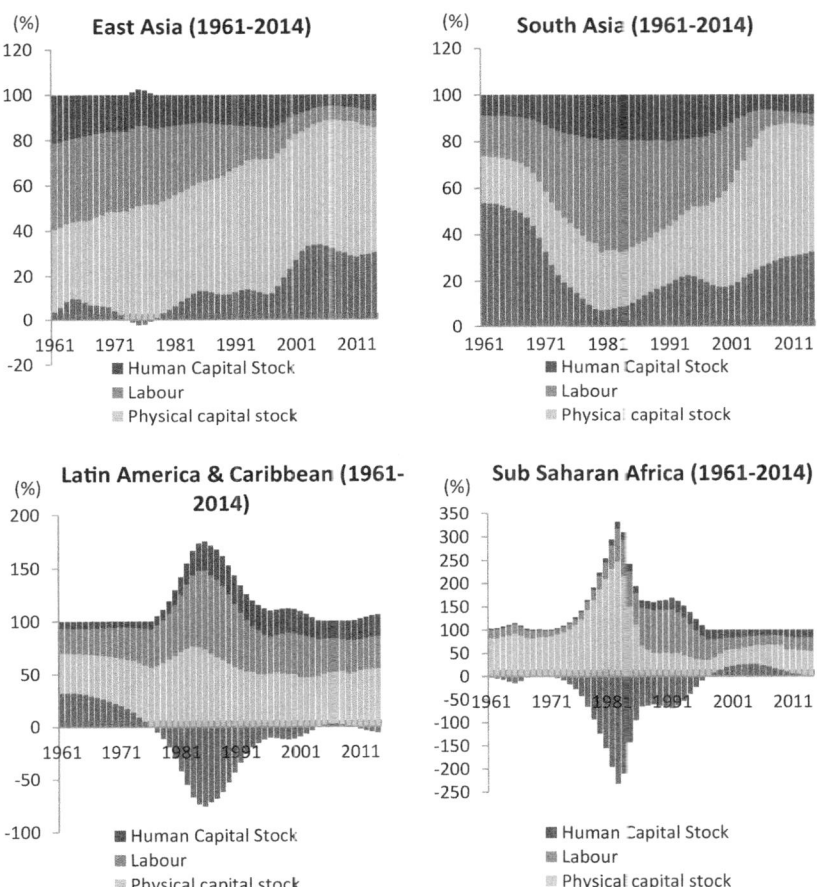

Fig. 3.3 Growth decomposition by factor, by region, 1970–present (change in growth = 100). *Source* Author's calculation based on Timmer et al. [2015]

that capital intensity is higher relative to other regions, and consequentially that growth is capital accumulation-led rather than labor productivity-led. Shares in the service sector in East Asia also saw a substantial rise over the period. The regional manufacturing shares for regions in Fig. 3.1 are consistent with what has been "premature deindustrialization" (a term credited to UNCTAD, 2003 and used by many others), in that developing countries have reached "peak manufacturing"

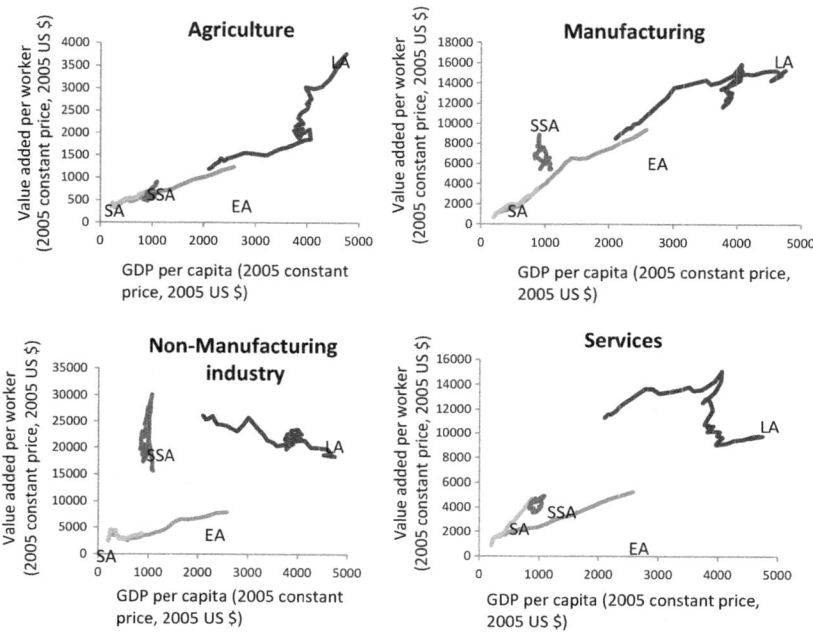

Fig. 3.4 Labor productivity versus GDP per capita, by region, 1960–present. *Source* Author's calculation based on Timmer et al. [2015]

in employment and value-added shares at a much earlier point in per capita income than the advanced nations.[2] Kaldor in his detailed empirical investigation on the relationship between manufacturing and growth concluded the UK was experiencing "premature maturity." This concept referred to an experience whereby manufacturing has "exhausted its growth potential before attaining particularly high levels of productivity or of average per capita income" (Kaldor 1978 [1966], p. 102). In contrast to manufacturing shares, service shares of GDP and employment are on an upward trend in general, particularly so in South Asia with a caveat that South Asia is represented by India alone in this estimation.[3]

Deindustrialization and tertiarization raise questions about the importance or otherwise of manufacturing as the driver of growth. In short, is manufacturing special as Kaldor outlined? Figure 3.2 estimates the sectoral sources of growth by region. These estimates are based on the method of Anand, Cheng, Rehman, and Zhang (2014) and show the decomposition of growth by sector (and factor–discussed next). The total

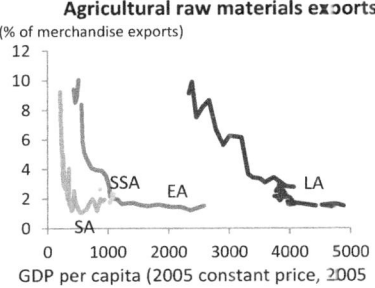
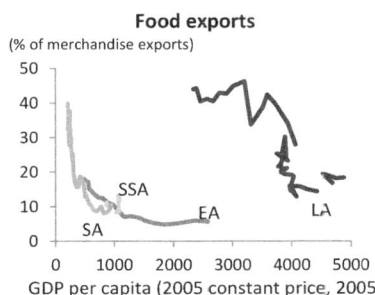
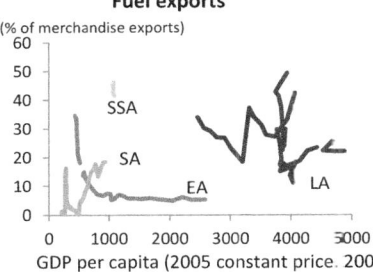
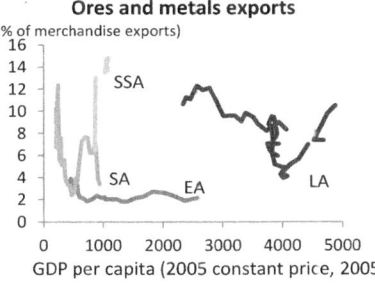
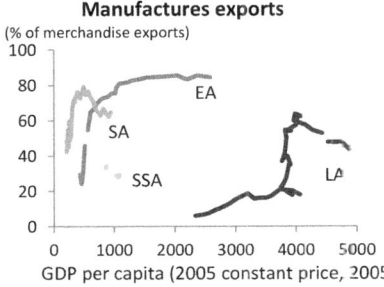
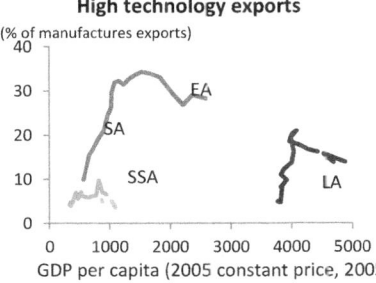

Fig. 3.5 Composition of exports by regions, 1960–present. *Source* Author's calculation based on Timmer et al [2015]

change in growth equals 100%. Figure 3.2 shows that growth in East Asia has been driven by an inter-sectoral movement toward manufacturing and away from agriculture over time. The contribution of nonmanufacturing industry and services has not changed much over the period. In contrast, services are a much more important contributor to growth in all other regions.

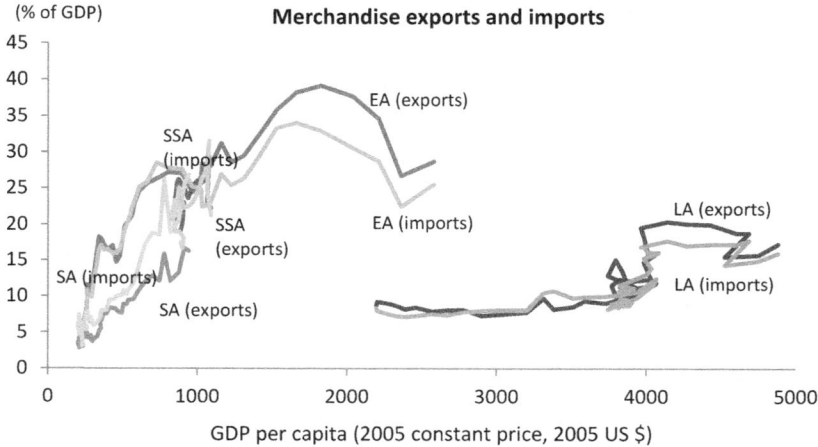

Fig. 3.6 Trade shares, 1961–present (or available years). *Source* Author's calculation based on Timmer et al. [2015]

Figure 3.3 make estimates of the decomposition of growth by factors of production. And Fig. 3.4 shows labour productivity trends. Figure 3.3 shows that capital accumulation (physical capital stock) played a major role in East Asia, and that role has been increasing over time which suggests an increase in the capital intensity of growth. Initially, this was mixed largely with labor input and human capital stock but as this diminished over time, total factor productivity (TFP) took a more significant role in growth.

In short, capital accumulation played a major role in East Asia over the entire period, while labor and human capital were gradually replaced with TFP from the mid-1980s onwards. In contrast, capital accumulation is relatively less important to growth in the other regions. In South Asia, capital accumulation becomes more important over time, whereas in sub-Saharan Africa it becomes less so. What is of interest here is the apparent either/or question of labor input and productivity. Growth is either physical capital plus labor absorption-driven or capital plus productivity-driven. This means that when TFP rises the labor input share tends to shrink and vice versa.[4]

Figure 3.4 shows labor productivity over the period by sector. It is not surprising to find a large increase in labor productivity in East Asia's manufacturing sector, given the inter-sectoral shifts away from agriculture to manufacturing. However, the labor productivity gains in other sectors are also significant, certainly in contrast to other regions where productivity has grown less or even fallen over the period.[5]

In terms of factors of production—labor in particular—demographic change is important. If we take the UN World Population Prospects (medium variant) we have estimates of the dependency ratio (the nonworking age population/working age population); the working age population (15–64 years) as a proportion of total population; and absolute changes (millions of people) in working age population. We find that the dependency ratio is falling in all regions and the working age population peaking in all regions with an exception to both in the case of sub-Saharan Africa. The sub-Saharan Africa curve lags somewhat, in that the trough of the dependency ratio curve will be experienced in all other regions by 2030–2050. In contrast, East Asia and Pacific, as well as Latin America and the Caribbean will face a shrinking labor force as sub-Saharan Africa is peaking.

Finally, integrative ST: Figs. 3.5 and 3.6 show the composition of exports and the trade balance Over the period, East Asia's exports show dramatic change over time. There are large declines in shares of agricultural raw material exports and food exports, and very rapid rises in shares of manufacturing exports and shares of high-tech exports. However, the plateauing of shares of manufacturing exports, and the peak and subsequent fall of shares of high-tech exports is cause for some alarm, given the importance of such exports to the region's economic development. The trends are consistent with a deindustrialization pattern. Perhaps surprisingly, despite economic development, the import shares show that East Asia still has a high proportion of import shares in manufactures, although this has fallen from a peak of 80% to approximately 60%. This is related to the phenomenon of manufacturing exports with corresponding high import content. If one looks across the overall trade position, only in East Asia is there a surplus for virtually the entire period. Latin America and sub-Saharan Africa both fluctuate from surpluses to deficits and back, and South Asia has a persistent trade deficit over the period.

3.2 The Characteristics of Contemporary Economic Development

In sum, over the period since the 1960s we can outline three stylized facts as follows: First, in all developing regions agriculture shares of GDP and employment have been falling substantially, though—surprisingly—employment shares in agriculture can persist at 40% of total employment up to $4000 per capita. This may simply be disguised under or unemployment though (or a statistical artefact). The rise in manufacturing shares in East Asia's GDP over the period is dramatic, though this is less the case for East Asia's manufacturing shares of employment. Further, the regional manufacturing shares are consistent with deindustrialization in employment shares and value-added though it is more a case of a plateau than a substantial downturn at least in the regional aggregates. It would appear even within the developing world the plateau is appearing earlier and earlier ($3000–$4000 for Latin America versus $1500 for East Asia). And service shares of GDP and employment are very much on an upward trend in general.

Second, growth in East Asia has been driven by an inter-sectoral movement toward manufacturing but services have been a much more important contributor to growth in all other regions. In East Asia capital accumulation (physical capital stock) played a major role and that role has been increasing over time which suggests an increase in the capital intensity of growth. In contrast, capital accumulation is relatively less important vis-à-vis other factors of production to growth in the other regions.

Third, while in East Asia there have been substantial changes in the composition exports—large falls of in shares of agricultural raw material exports and food exports, and rises in shares of manufacturing exports and shares of high-tech exports—this is not the case elsewhere. That said, in East Asia there is a visible plateauing of shares of manufactures in exports, and there is a peak and subsequent fall of shares of high-tech manufactures shares of exports. Persistent trade surpluses appear to be regionally elusive outside East Asia. In both Latin America and sub-Saharan Africa the trade position fluctuates from surpluses to deficits and back and South Asia has a persistent deficit for all of the period under study.

NOTES

1. One general limitation of any such measures is specifically, as Fischer (2011, 2014) discusses whether productivity can be accurately measured in a complex economy give that measuring productivity relies on value-added account data, but such data is a combination of output and prices/wages. So, most measurements for productivity show price or wage differentials not actual effort, output, or skill. This is an even bigger problem in the service sector as the comparability of services is more problematic because

they are not physical goods that can be compared. Fischer (2014) also notes another problem that, because transnational companies (TNCs)—who dominate production and its coordination in global value chains—conduct practices such as transfer pricing and the transferring of profits from Southern subsidiaries to Northern HQs (for example, low-interest loans from subsidiary to parent company), such actions could make the subsidiary look less productive. These are clearly important issues that, although not easily resolved, should not be forgotten.

2. See also Dasgupta and Singh (2006), Heintz (2009), Rowthorn and Ramaswamy (1999), Amirapu and Subramanian (2015). Lewis (1979, p. 220) notes that "the surest way to run into trouble is to have 'de-industrialization' (industrial employment growing more slowly than the labor force), since this means that the reservoir or cheap labor will be filling instead of emptying. The political and social health of the community, no less its economic health, requires a continual transfer from the reservoir to the more productive sectors, rather than the relative expansion of the reservoir."

3. We construct regional aggregates as follows: East Asia includes China, Indonesia, Malaysia, Philippines, and Thailand; South Asia includes India; Latin America includes Argentina, Bolivia, Brazil, Colombia, Costa Rica, Mexico, Peru, and Venezuela; Sub-Saharan Africa includes Botswana, Ethiopia, Ghana, Kenya, Malawi, Nigeria, Senegal, South Africa, and Tanzania.

4. In the graphs, the labor and human capital accumulation contribution is smaller (or the physical capital contribution share is larger) than in Anand et al. (2014) because they assume (22), as does Kaldor (1957), that the labor share is constant at two-thirds across all countries and all years. This is based on Cobb-Douglas (1928) who argued empirically (based on the United States) that labor shares are static, as labor is paid according to its own productivity (see Douglas 1976). However, when one takes the labor shares from the latest Penn World Tables we find that the labor share ranges substantially. For example, in 2005, from a minimum of 0.18 to a maximum of 0.89 and a mean of 0.52 in 2005. Thus, of the set of countries we use here, the labor share is much lower than the commonly thought two-thirds share for most years, and therefore the labor share is a smaller contributor and the capital share is a bigger contributor if one takes into account the actual labor shares.

5. This is an alternative view on the "middle-income trap" debate. Rather than seek to plot a growth slow-down, the figure plots productivity growth versus GDP per capita and demonstrates a middle-income trap as a productivity slow-down in Latin America in all sectors but agriculture.

REFERENCES

Amirapu, A., & Subramanian, A. (2015). *Manufacturing or services? An Indian illustration of a development dilemma* (Center for Global Development Working Paper 409). Washington, DC: CGD.

Anand, R., Cheng, K. C., Rehman, S., & Zhang, L. (2014). *Potential growth in emerging Asia* (IMF Working Paper). Washington, DC: IMF.

Dasgupta, S., & Singh, A. (2006). *Manufacturing, services and premature deindustrialisation in developing countries: A Kaldorian analysis* (UNU-WIDER, United Nations University Research Paper, No. 2006/49). Helsinki: UNU-WIDER.

Diao, X., McMillan, M., Rodrik, D., & Kennedy, J. F. (2017). *The recent growth boom in developing economies: A structural-change perspective* (NBER Working Paper Series No. 23132). Cambridge, MA: NBER. Retrieved from http://www.nber.org/papers/w23132.

Douglas, P. H. (1976). The Cobb-Douglas production function once again: Its history, its testing, and some empirical values. *Journal of Political Economy, 84*(5), 903–915.

Duarte, M., & Restuccia, D. (2010). The role of the structural transformation in aggregate productivity. *The Quarterly Journal of Economics, 125*(1), 129–173.

Fischer, A. (2011). Beware the fallacy of productivity reductionism. *The European Journal of Development Research, 23*(4), 521–526.

Fischer, A. M. (2014). *The social value of employment and the redistributive imperative for development* (UNDP Human Development Report Office, Occasional Paper). New York: UNDP.

Gollin, D. (2014). The Lewis model: A 60-year retrospective. *Journal of Economic Perspectives, 28*(3), 71–88.

Heintz, J. (2009). *Employment, economic development and poverty reduction: Critical issues and policy challenges.* Geneva: UNRISD.

Kaldor, N. (1978 [1966]). *Causes of the slow rate of economic growth of the United Kingdom.* Cambridge: Cambridge University Press.

Lewis, W. A. (1979). The dual economy revisited. *The Manchester School, 47*(3): 211–229.

Rowthorn, R., & Ramaswamy, R. (1999). *Growth, trade, and deindustrialization* (IMF Staff Papers). Washington, DC: IMF.

Timmer, M. P., de Vries, G. J., & de Vries, K. (2015). Patterns of structural change in developing countries. In J. Weiss & M. A. Tribe (Eds.), *Routledge handbook of industry and development* (pp. 65–83). London: Routledge.

Open Access This chapter is licensed under the terms of the Creative Commons Attribution 4.0 International License (http://creativecommons.org/licenses/by/4.0/), which permits use, sharing, adaptation, distribution and reproduction in any medium or format, as long as you give appropriate credit to the original author(s) and the source, provide a link to the Creative Commons license and indicate if changes were made.

The images or other third party material in this chapter are included in the chapter's Creative Commons license, unless indicated otherwise in a credit line to the material. If material is not included in the chapter's Creative Commons license and your intended use is not permitted by statutory regulation or exceeds the permitted use, you will need to obtain permission directly from the copyright holder.

PART II

The Future of Economic Development, Work and Wages in the Developing World

CHAPTER 4

Technological Transformation

Abstract Most research on the economic implications of automation has so far focused on advanced industrialized economies where the cost of labor is high and manufacturing shows a high degree of mechanization and productivity. Yet, the developing world is likely to be both affected by automation trends in high-income countries (HICs) and is itself catching up in terms of automation. "Late developers" are facing the digital revolution earlier and under different conditions than today's advanced economies. There is an increasing worry that any low-cost labor advantage of developing countries in international trade is eroding. Beyond the alarmist threat of "technological unemployment," there are broader questions to be asked about how automation and digitization influence global economic development, employment growth, and structural transformation.

Keywords Automation · Robots · Artificial intelligence · Digital revolution · Technological adoption · Automatability

4.1 Contemporary Technological Trends

Stunning technological advances in robotics and artificial intelligence (AI) are being reported virtually on a daily basis: from the versatile mobile robots of the US engineering company *Boston Dynamics* to

© The Author(s) 2020
L. Schlogl and A. Sumner, *Disrupted Development and the Future of Inequality in the Age of Automation*, Rethinking International Development series, https://doi.org/10.1007/978-3-030-30131-6_4

autonomous vehicles, vessels, and drones, to 3D-printed buildings and new breakthroughs in machine learning made by firms in the Silicon Valley and beyond. A growing number of empirical studies and several monographs have recently addressed the broader phenomenon of a "digital revolution" which is unfolding at high speed across OECD countries. Interest in the impact of technological change is by no means new of course as the detailed empirical study of Leontief and Duchin (1984) is testimony to. Indeed, one can trace the subject back to the classical writings of David Ricardo (2010 [1817]) and Karl Marx (2012 [1867]) or Joseph Schumpeter (1943). The bulk of research on the economic implications of digital transformation has so far focused on advanced industrialized economies where the cost of labor is high and manufacturing shows a high degree of mechanization and productivity. Yet, the developing world is both affected by automation trends in high-income countries (HICs) and is itself catching up in terms of automation.

Indicative of this, the International Federation of Robotics (IFR) reports that Asia is currently the "strongest growth market" in a "significant rise in demand for industrial robots worldwide" (IFR, 2016, pp. 11f.). A double-digit growth trend includes not only China, Korea, and Japan but also emerging economies in South East Asia. The IFR (2016) estimates that by 2019, more than 250,000 units of multipurpose industrial robots will be installed in Asia on a yearly basis, with the main industries driving demand in robots being the automotive, electrical/electronics, metal, and machinery, as well as the rubber and plastics industries. This only captures the more easily measurable demand for robotics hardware and does not take account of the widespread use of software in the context of economic production. In some domains of automation, emerging economies are, in fact, ahead of many OECD countries, as the opening of Beijing's first driverless subway line in 2017 (Yan, 2017) or the popularity of the mobile phone-based financing platform M-Pesa in Kenya illustrate.

The digitization and automation of economies raises the question of what lessons the developing world can draw from extant evidence. "Late developers" are facing the digital revolution considerably earlier and under different conditions than today's advanced economies. There is thus an increasing worry that "increased automation in low-wage countries, which have traditionally attracted manufacturing firms, could see them lose their cost advantage and potentially lose their ability of achieving rapid economic growth by shifting workers to factory jobs" which today's HICs used to have (Frey, Osborne, & Holmes, 2016). Beyond the perceived threat of "technological unemployment," there are broader questions to be asked about how automation and digitization influence economic development, employment growth, and structural transformation in developing countries. It may well be that labor displacement is less of an issue than real-wage growth as a result of the potential for automation, for example.

4.2 Automation: Definitions and Determinants

The concept of automation is more difficult to define than might seem at first glance. Throughout history, humans have used tools to save time and effort when completing laborious tasks and thanks to innovation, such tools have gradually increased in sophistication. Today, the spectrum of "physical capital" ranges from simple manual tools to intelligent machines. One could thus argue that a "robot" is simply a highly advanced version of a tool which requires minimal (manual) human input for completing a task, although currently all machines still require considerable human intervention in their design, production, installation, and maintenance. The potential of AI is to move machines beyond human oversight, at least in everyday operation. An intelligent machine performs a set of complex tasks autonomously and may be capable of adapting to new and changing circumstances, i.e. "learning." Workhorse animals could be considered a biological equivalent of complex machines and have been used in transportation and agriculture since at least the agricultural revolution in 10,000 BC. Contemporary automation often tends to be associated with physical hardware such as industrial robots, but also includes software which plays a critical role in service automation (see Lacity & Willcocks, 2018; Willcocks & Lacity, 2016). The wider process of structural economic change toward an automated economy has been referred to not only as a digital transformation but as the "fourth industrial revolution" (Schwab, 2016).

Under what conditions might such a transformation or revolution take place? Technological feasibility is just *one* condition. Table 4.1 shows multiple criteria which the decision to automate involves: can a task be automated in a way that reliably produces a good or service at a specified level of quality? Is it profitable to automate that task? Is it legally possible for a firm to replace workers with machines? How do relevant stakeholders such as political groupings, particularly trade unions, and

Table 4.1 Determinants of the feasibility of automation

Dimension	Factors	Literature
Technological	Type and complexity of the task	Engineering studies, "jobs at risk" studies (e.g. Arntz, Gregory, & Zierahn, 2016; Grace, Salvatier, Dafoe, Zhang, & Evans, 2017; McKinsey Global Institute, 2017a)
Economic	Economic risks and returns given capital and labor costs; intensity of competition	Management/human resources and economics literature (e.g. Hall & Khan, 2003; Siegel, Waldman, & Youngdahl, 1997)
Legal	Labor and capital regulation (e.g. job protection); patents and their ownership	Institutionalism and political economy (e.g. Acemoglu & Robinson, 2000; Parente & Prescott, 1994; Williams & Edge, 1996)
Political	e.g. unionization of the workforce; questions of public versus private ownership of production and technology	
Sociocultural	e.g. corporate legitimacy and social expectations	

Source Authors and references cited

society at large, particularly consumers, respond to automation (and the potentially ensuing lay-offs)?

Corresponding to these criteria, one could split the literature on automation into different theoretical approaches. Much recent research has focused on the first criterion in Table 4.1: the technological feasibility of automation. Yet, automatable tasks do not necessarily or instantly get automated: one can observe a set of tasks currently being carried out both by humans and machines in different contexts and places. Consider, for instance, subway drivers and autonomous subways, supermarket cashiers, and self-checkout machines, university lecturers, and online courses. The coexistence of automated and nonautomated modes of operation of the same task suggests that a narrowly technologically deterministic view is insufficient. There are less tangible—economic, political, social, and cultural—reasons to be factored in. Such factors up until now often seem to have been neglected in research on automation, but could be particularly important in the context of developing countries. Such factors not only determine if automation occurs but the terms of automation vis-à-vis governing institutions.

Consider, for example, the case of Indonesia. In Indonesia, there have been numerous media reports related to automation and employment impacts (e.g. Deny, 2017; *Jakarta Globe*, 2017; Jefriando, 2017; Praditya, 2017; Saragih, 2017; *Tempo*, 2015, 2016a, 2016b, 2016c, 2017; see also international press such as *The Guardian*, 2016). The McKinsey Global Institute (2017b) estimates that around half of all jobs in Indonesia are automatable using existing technologies. One example is that motorway toll booths are being automated to an e-payment system which has placed a question over 20,000 jobs, leading the Minister of Finance to announce at the annual meeting of the International Monetary Fund and the World Bank that automation might create a case for a future universal basic income in Indonesia (*Jakarta Post*, 2017; Jefriando, 2017).

While formerly each tollgate required five employees working in shifts to ensure vehicles had paid the road toll, the cashless system which is being rolled out runs entirely without human operators, thus speeding up the transaction process and reducing traffic congestion. Yet, as of early 2018, the toll road operator PT Jasa Marga asserts that "former tollgate keepers would instead be relocated to different positions within the company (…) and would keep their permanent employee status" (Aisyah, 2017).

There have, indeed, so far, been no reports of mass lay-offs despite the electronic system being implemented. What could be the reason? First, it could be that, as implementation is still in an early stage, lay-offs may be a matter of time, and could happen in a gradual manner. The company may also reduce its future intake of new employees as a result. Second, it could be that, in line with the quote above, PT Jasa Marga, which is currently expanding its business, truly has the capacity to absorb 20,000 people in other sectors of its operation. If that is the case, this raises the important question as to whether by raising overall productivity and competitiveness, automation somehow allowed the company to expand. The latter would mean that automation has the double effect of reducing labor demand per unit of capital in one domain (e.g. manual toll collection) while raising labor demand in complementary domains (e.g. administrative or construction tasks).

Finally, there is a set of institutional reasons that could be an important explanatory factor as to why PT Jasa Marga—a state-owned enterprise and thus facing potential developmental obligations—has not laid off workers: political and social-norms pressures as well as legal constraints could be preventing the toll road operator from firing employees. One could imagine the political backlash of a state-owned enterprise making 20,000 people unemployed. There may be also concerns over strikes, attacks on the new toll-booth machinery, political interventions (including fears of the political replacement of senior management making such decisions) or negative media reports which demonstrably influence business decisions in part of wholly owned SOEs and to some extent in private companies too.

4.3 Theoretical Perspectives on Automation

One could crudely distinguish the existing scholarly literature on automation and digitization effects into two camps: first, there is an optimists' camp which essentially sees the "business as usual" of market dynamism at work. Technological change, they argue, has been an essential element of "modern economic growth" since the Industrial Revolution, and disruptive innovation has always been met with what Mokyr, Vickers, and Ziebarth (2015) call "technological anxiety." This has been the case at least since the arrival of the steam engine and the power loom. Simon Kuznets (1971) in his Nobel lecture argued that the most important feature of modern economic growth is a "combination of a high rate of aggregate growth with disrupting effects and new 'problems'." Such disruption refers, in particular, to changes in the economic and social structure that technological innovation generates.

Joseph Schumpeter, key theorist of technological innovation, famously coined the notion of "creative destruction" for the "process of industrial mutation that incessantly revolutionizes the economic structure *from within*, incessantly destroying the old one, incessantly creating a new one" and called this the "essential fact about capitalism" (Schumpeter, 1943, pp. 42f., emphasis in original). Schumpeter's view on the economics of technology in the context of the Industrial Revolution preceded the neoclassical standard model of growth advanced by Solow (1956). In his aggregate production function, Solow attributed all output growth not accounted for by increases in capital and/or labor to a broad category of "technical change" (Granstrand, 1994, p. 13).

Scholars in this optimistic tradition thus tend to emphasize the historically demonstrated adaptive capacity of market economies to innovation and change with little emphasis on any temporary or permanent "losers" in the process. Further, they argue that robots and computers take over repetitive, dangerous, unhealthy tasks, and so improve both the quality of work and of products and come with public health benefits. Importantly, automation decreases the cost of production and should thus, in a competitive market, lead to lower prices which benefit all consumers. Not only this, but "automation, by reducing wages relative to the rental rate of capital, encourages the creation of new labor-intensive tasks and generates a powerful self-correcting force towards stability" (Acemoglu & Restrepo, 2015, p. 41). Optimists tend to suggest skills development for the labor force to allow a synergetic relationship of human and nonhuman work. This is in keeping with Goldin and Katz' (2007) race between technology and skill supply itself drawing on the Tinbergen (1974, 1975) thesis. Further, they might advocate to reduce taxes on labor which would make labor relatively more competitive vis-à-vis robots.

The pessimists' camp, on the other hand, argues that "this time it's different": contemporary iterations of automation and digitization are viewed as being part of a larger "digital revolution" (Avent, 2017) which is bringing about technologies that are more powerful and versatile than earlier iterations of the Industrial Revolution, and which will wholly or partially replace *human brains* rather than just the *human muscle* replaced by earlier technologies. The digital revolution, it is argued, is creating an array of intelligent, adaptive, general-purpose technologies with hitherto unseen labor-saving potentials for a widening group of tasks. This group of tasks increasingly includes complex, skill-intensive work and formerly hard-to-automate manual work like stitching. The relationship of human and nonhuman work is viewed as more and more *substitutive* rather than *complementary*. In this vein, an in-depth report of the Executive Office of the President of the United States (2016, p. 22) commissioned by Barack Obama warns that "the skills in which humans have maintained a comparative advantage are likely to erode over time as AI and new technologies become more sophisticated." DeLong (2015) argues too that, just like horses once used to dominate economic production, human labor currently dominates it, but that "peak human" may have been reached.

Pessimists argue that automation is putting a downward pressure on wages (reflected in stagnating real wages) and an upward pressure on the rate of profit from capital investment. The detachment of productivity gains and wage growth observed since the 1970s in many OECD countries is brought forward as evidence. Automation, pessimists argue, may ultimately lead to job losses as technologies create fewer jobs than they eliminate ("technological unemployment") or create jobs in sectors which are potentially less desirable and productive ("premature deindustrialization"). Politically, the recommendations of the pessimist camp range from a "robot tax" to redistributive responses such as a universal basic income (with the latter potentially funded by the former) and questions of public versus private ownership of production and technology.

It is fair to say that the second, more pessimistic, camp has been increasingly visible in recent years. Yet, unemployment is generally not considered to be the main issue. With a view to the United States, economic experts from the IGM Panel (2014) agree that automation has not (yet) markedly reduced employment but has rather led to a stagnation of median wages, a decoupling of real-wage growth from productivity growth, and a labor market polarization or "hollowing out" of middle-skill employment. Technology can depress or enhance wage growth depending on whether it substitutes or complements tasks (see for discussion, Acemoglu & Autor, 2011; Autor, Katz, & Kearney, 2004; Firpo, Fortin, & Lemieux, 2011; Goos & Manning, 2007).

Further, it should not be taken as given that lower skilled work will necessarily be automated, but it can contribute to a "missing middle" whereby most jobs are low or high skilled, and those in-between are relatively more susceptible to automation, or whereby employment expansion in those middle-skill jobs is weaker than that of low- and high-skilled jobs (see Autor, Levy, & Murnane, 2003). The problem thus may not be so much that jobs are lost, rather than that other types of jobs expand in number. People are being driven into the jobs below their skill level, with either lower or slower growing wages than the middle-skill jobs that previously existed.

A key question is what happens to productivity growth in any given country. In short, who "captures" the productivity growth in terms of capital or labor and the functional distribution of income. And how what is captured is then distributed within the capital share (which may be distributed between reinvestment, dividend payments, reserves building, or other activity e.g. rents), or within the labor share which may be distributed between employment growth, real-wage growth, or social security entitlements (see discussion of Atkinson, 2009; Francese & Mulas-Granados, 2015). This matters from an individual income inequality perspective, as reductions in the labor share of income are correlated with rising income inequality between individuals (see for detailed discussion, Chapter 3 of IMF, 2017).

References

Acemoglu, D., & Autor, D. (2011). Skills, tasks and technologies: Implications for employment and earnings. In O. Ashenfelter & D. Card (Eds.), *Handbook of labor economics* (Vol. 4B, pp. 1043–1171). Amsterdam: Elsevier.

Acemoglu, D., & Restrepo, P. (2015). The race between machine and man: Implications of technology for growth, factor shares and employment. *SSRN Electronic Journal*. https://doi.org/10.2139/ssrn.2781320.

Acemoglu, D., & Robinson, J. A. (2000). Political losers as a barrier to economic development. *American Economic Review Papers and Proceedings, 90*, 126–130.

Aisyah, R. (2017, November 3). No layoffs after full cashless payment: Toll road operator. *The Jakarta Post*. Retrieved from http://www.thejakartapost.com/news/2017/11/03/no-layoffs-after-full-cashless-payment-toll-road-operator.html.

Arntz, M., Gregory, T., & Zierahn, U. (2016). The risk of automation for jobs in OECD countries: A comparative analysis. *OECD Social, Employment and Migration Working Papers, 2*(189), 47–54.

Atkinson, A. B. (2009). Factor shares: The principal problem of political economy. *Oxford Review of Economic Policy, 25*(1), 3–16.

Autor, D. H., Katz, L. F., & Kearney, M. S. (2004). The polarization of the U.S. labor market. *AEA Papers and Proceedings, 96*(2), 189–194.

Autor, D. H., Levy, F., & Murnane, R. J. (2003). The skill content of recent technological change: An empirical exploration. *The Quarterly Journal of Economics, 118*(4), 1279–1333.

Avent, R. (2017). *The wealth of humans: Work and its absence in the twenty-first century*. London: Penguin Random House.

DeLong, B. (2015). *Technological progress anxiety: Thinking about "peak horse" and the possibility of "peak human"*. Retrieved from http://equitablegrowth.org/equitablog/technological-progress-anxiety-thinking-about-peak-horse-and-the-possibility-of-peak-human/.

Deny, S. (2017, August 24). Sri mulyani khawatir generasi muda ri kalah dengan robot. *Liputan 6*. Retrieved from http://bisnis.liputan6.com/read/3069606/sri-mulyani-khawatir-generasi-muda-ri-kalah-dengan-robot.

Executive Office of the President of the United States. (2016). *Preparing for the future of artificial intelligence*. Washington, DC. Retrieved from https://obamawhitehouse.archives.gov/sites/default/files/whitehouse_files/microsites/ostp/NSTC/preparing_for_the_future_of_ai.pdf.

Firpo, S. P., Fortin, N. M., & Lemieux, T. (2011). *Occupational tasks and changes in the wage structure* (IZA Discussion Paper No. 5542). Bonn: IZA. Retrieved from ftp.iza.org/dp5542.pdf.

Francese, M., & Mulas-Granados, C. (2015). *Functional income distribution and its role in explaining inequality* (IMF Working Papers 15/244). Washington, DC: IMF. Retrieved from https://www.imf.org/en/Publications/WP/Issues/2016/12/31/Functional-Income-Distribution-and-Its-Role-in-Explaining-Inequality-43415.

Frey, C. B., Osborne, M. A., & Holmes, C. (2016). *Technology at work v2.0: The future is not what it used to be* (Citi GPS: Global Perspectives & Solutions). Oxford. Retrieved from http://www.oxfordmartin.ox.ac.uk/downloads/reports/Citi_GPS_Technology_Work_2.pdf.

Goldin, C., & Katz, L. F. (2007). *The race between education and technology: The evolution of U.S. educational wage differentials, 1890 to 2005* (NBER Working Paper Series No. 12984). Cambridge, MA: NBER. Retrieved from http://www.nber.org/papers/w12984.

Goos, M., & Manning, A. (2007). Lousy and lovely jobs: The rising polarization of work in Britain. *Review of Economics and Statistics, 89*(1), 118–133.

Grace, K., Salvatier, J., Dafoe, A., Zhang, B., & Evans, O. (2017). *When will AI exceed human performance? Evidence from AI experts* (arXiv No. 1705.08807v2). Retrieved from http://arxiv.org/abs/1705.08807.

Granstrand, O. (1994). *Economics of technology*. Amsterdam: North-Holland.

Hall, B. H., & Khan, B. (2003). *Adoption of new technology* (NBER Working Paper Series No. 9730). Cambridge, MA: NBER. Retrieved from http://www.nber.org/papers/w9730.

IFR. (2016). *Executive summary: World robotics 2016 service robots* (International Federation of Robotics). Retrieved from http://www.ifr.org/fileadmin/user_upload/downloads/World_Robotics/2016/Executive_Summary_WR_Industrial_Robots_2016.pdf.

IGM Panel. (2014, February 25). Robots. *IGM Forum*. Retrieved from http://www.igmchicago.org/surveys/robots.

IMF. (2017). *World economic outlook, April 2017: Gaining momentum?* Washington, DC: IMF. Retrieved from http://www.imf.org/en/Publications/WEO/Issues/2017/04/04/world-economic-outlook-april-2017.

Jakarta Globe. (2017, October 13). Indonesia to consider universal basic income. *Jakarta Globe*. Retrieved from http://jakartaglobe.id/business/indonesia-to-study-universal-basic-income/.

Jakarta Post. (2017, September 14). Non-cash toll will affect 10,000 workers in Jakarta. *The Jakarta Post*. Retrieved from http://www.thejakartapost.com/news/2017/09/14/non-cash-toll-will-affect-10000-workers-in-jakarta.html.

Jefriando, M. (2017, October 12). Sri mulyani bicara soal robot ancam pekerjaan manusia. *Detik*. Retrieved from https://finance.detik.com/berita-ekonomi-bisnis/3680492/sri-mulyani-bicara-soal-robot-ancam-pekerjaan-manusia.

Kuznets, S. (1971). *Modern economic growth: Findings and reflections: Lecture to the memory of Alfred Nobel*. Stockholm: The Nobel Foundation. Retrieved from http://www.nobelprize.org/nobel_prizes/economic-sciences/laureates/1971/kuznets-lecture.html.

Lacity, M., & Willcocks, L. P. (2018). *Robotic process and cognitive automation: The next phase*. Stratford: Steve Brookes Publishing.

Leontief, W., & Duchin, F. (1984). The impacts of automation on employment, 1963–2000. *CATESOL Journal, 5*(1), 1963–2000. Retrieved from http://files.eric.ed.gov/fulltext/ED241743.pdf.

Marx, K. (2012 [1867]). *Das Kapital: A critique of political economy*. Washington, DC: Regnery Publishing.

McKinsey Global Institute. (2017a). *A future that works: Automation, employment, and productivity*. Retrieved from https://www.mckinsey.com/~/media/McKinsey/Global%20Themes/Digital%20Disruption/Harnessing%20automation%20for%20a%20future%20that%20works/MGI-A-future-that-works_Full-report.ashx.

McKinsey Global Institute. (2017b). *Where machines could replace humans—And where they can't (yet)*. Retrieved from https://public.tableau.com/en-us/s/gallery/where-machines-could-replace-humans.

Mokyr, J., Vickers, C., & Ziebarth, N. L. (2015). The history of technological anxiety and the future of economic growth: Is this time different? *Journal of Economic Perspectives, 29*(3), 31–50.

Parente, S. L., & Prescott, E. C. (1994). Barriers to technology adoption and development. *Journal of Political Economy, 102*(2), 298–321.

Praditya, I. I. (2017, August 17). 72 tahun merdeka, ri masih hadapi deindustrialisasi. *Liputan 6*. Retrieved from http://bisnis.liputan6.com/read/3061377/72-tahun-merdeka-ri-masih-hadapi-deindustrialisasi.

Ricardo, D. (2010). *On the principles of political economy, and taxation*. Urbana, Illinois: Project Gutenberg. http://www.gutenberg.org/files/33310/33310-h/33310-h.htm.

Saragih, F. A. (2017, September 16). Otomatisasi tol dianggap kejahatan. *Kompas.com*. Retrieved from http://ekonomi.kompas.com/read/2017/09/16/080100530/otomatisasi-tol-dianggap-kejahatan.

Schumpeter, J. A. (1943). *Capitalism, socialism and democracy*. Abingdon-on-Thames: Routledge.

Schwab, K. (2016). *The fourth industrial revolution*. Geneva: Portfolio Penguin.

Siegel, D. S., Waldman, D. A., & Youngdahl, W. E. (1997). The adoption of advanced manufacturing technologies: Human resource management implications. *IEEE Transactions on Engineering Management, 44*(3), 288–298.

Solow, R. M. (1956). A contribution to the theory of economic growth. *The Quarterly Journal of Economics, 70*(1), 65–94.

Tempo. (2015, December 14). Provinsi di Indonesia ini alami gejala deindustrialisasi. *Tempo.co.* Retrieved from https://bisnis.tempo.co/read/727694/provinsi-di-indonesia-ini-alami-gejala-deindustrialisasi.
Tempo. (2016a, January 12). Bali bans the operation of Uber Taxi. *Tempo.co.* Retrieved from https://en.tempo.co/read/news/2016/01/21/056738210/Bali-Bans-the-Operation-of-Uber-Taxi.
Tempo. (2016b, March 21). Protes Uber dan Grab, sopir se-Jakarta akan unjuk rasa. *Tempo.co.* Retrieved from https://metro.tempo.co/read/755352/protes-uber-dan-grab-sopir-se-jakarta-akan-unjuk-rasa.
Tempo. (2016c, September 27). 200 Ribu pekerja terancam phk karena otomatisasi gardu tol. *Tempo.co.* Retrieved from https://bisnis.tempo.co/read/807738/200-ribu-pekerja-terancam-phk-karena-otomatisasi-gardu-tol.
Tempo. (2017, February 20). Era Digital, jumlah pengangguran meningkat. *Tempo.co.* Retrieved from https://tekno.tempo.co/read/848320/era-digital-jumlah-pengangguran-meningkat.
The Guardian. (2016, March 22). Traffic chaos and violence as thousands of taxi drivers protest against Uber in Jakarta. *The Guardian.* Retrieved from https://www.theguardian.com/world/2016/mar/22/traffic-chaos-and-violence-as-thousands-of-taxi-drivers-protest-uber-in-jakarta.
Tinbergen, J. (1974). Substitution of graduate by other labour. *Kyklos, 27*(2), 217–226.
Tinbergen, J. (1975). Substitution of academically trained by other manpower. *Review of World Economics, 111*(3), 466–476.
Willcocks, Leslie P., & Lacity, Mary. (2016). *Service automation: Robots and the future of work.* Stratford: Steve Brookes Publishing.
Williams, R., & Edge, D. (1996). The social shaping of technology. *Research Policy, 25*(6), 865–899.
Yan, A. (2017, June 12). Beijing's first driverless subway line starts test run. *CGTN.* Retrieved from https://news.cgtn.com/news/3d557a4d3249444e/share_p.html.

Open Access This chapter is licensed under the terms of the Creative Commons Attribution 4.0 International License (http://creativecommons.org/licenses/by/4.0/), which permits use, sharing, adaptation, distribution and reproduction in any medium or format, as long as you give appropriate credit to the original author(s) and the source, provide a link to the Creative Commons license and indicate if changes were made.

The images or other third party material in this chapter are included in the chapter's Creative Commons license, unless indicated otherwise in a credit line to the material. If material is not included in the chapter's Creative Commons license and your intended use is not permitted by statutory regulation or exceeds the permitted use, you will need to obtain permission directly from the copyright holder.

CHAPTER 5

Automation and Structural Transformation in Developing Countries

Abstract Technological change is likely to create a dual economy of automation-resistant and automation-susceptible sectors. Correspondingly, the labor force employed in automatable domains is pushed toward new activities—a dynamic that we liken to the classical Lewis model. We argue that the role of artificial intelligence and other advances is likely to be what we term a "robot reserve army," providing infinite supplies of artificial labor particularly in the agricultural and manufacturing sector. From this emerges a new pattern of structural transformation, as outlined in the previous chapter, with new distributional implications. We argue that tertiarization, income inequality, and wage stagnation, rather than, technological unemployment, are the key challenges of late development in the age of automation.

Keywords Robot reserve army · Lewis model 2.0 · Automatability · Employment · Distribution · Tertiarization

5.1 Characteristics of Developing Countries

Developing countries have special characteristics (vis-à-vis OECD countries): they tend to be labor-abundant and have higher rates of population growth than OECD countries. Large proportions of the population are often relatively unskilled and tertiary education is still comparatively

© The Author(s) 2020
L. Schlogl and A. Sumner, *Disrupted Development and the Future of Inequality in the Age of Automation*, Rethinking International Development series, https://doi.org/10.1007/978-3-030-30131-6_5

limited even in upper middle-income developing countries. Compared to advanced high-income countries, they have a larger agricultural sector, and lower employment and value-added shares in industry and manufacturing, as well as a large informal service sector again not only in the world's poorest countries but even in upper middle-income countries. Production in such economies is less capital-intensive and productivity levels are thus lower than in high-income countries.

A number of developing countries have substantially shifted economic value-added activity from agriculture and resources to manufacturing and service sectors. For developing countries with such characteristics, a set of questions arises in the context of automation (that are different to the world's very poorest countries): What if industrial production can increasingly be carried out with minimal human labor input? What if robots in high-income countries start to compete with cheap labor? Is it plausible that there could be a disintegration of global value chains via "reshoring," i.e. the repatriation of formerly outsourced production to high-income countries? What if the service sector—where currently the largest share of labor is absorbed in many middle-income developing countries—goes through dramatic shifts of labor productivity, thanks to innovations in software and AI? Does automation exacerbate a much-debated "middle-income trap" if it exists at all and thus impede catch-up development? Are there new sectors of economic activity emerging which promise decent employment opportunities for large populations rather than economic growth accompanied by weak employment growth? These questions point toward the importance of situating the role of technology in broader theories of economic development.

5.2 Disrupted Development? The Role of Technological Change in Long-Run Economic Development

The neoclassical standard model of growth attributes a key role to technological change in long-run economic growth. In the Solow (1956) model, growth can be achieved either via an increase in the inputs of production, e.g. an expansion of the labor force or an increase in the capital intensity, or it can happen via greater efficiency in the combination of inputs that generates a larger output. The latter route is known as the dynamics of total factor productivity (TFP) and innovation in automation technologies is generally considered an important factor in raising the TFP.

Summers (2013) considers a modification of the neoclassical two-factor production function in which output is created via both a *complementary* and a *substitutive* use of capital and labor (see for discussion Atkinson & Bourguignon, 2014, p. xilx). Capital will be "deployed in these two uses to the point where their marginal productivity is the same" (Summers, 2013, p. 4) and a certain mix of capital and labor will result. Summers highlights three implications of labor-saving capital use: (i) production opportunities are augmented and output thus increases; (ii) wage rates fall; and (iii) returns to capital rise. Atkinson and Bourguignon thus argue:

> We can therefore tell a story of macroeconomic development where initially the Solow model apples (...). A rising capital-labor ratio leads to rising wages and a falling rate of return. Beyond a certain point however (...) [labor-substituting capital use] begins to be positive. We then see further growth in the economy, as capital per head rises (...). There is no longer any gain to wage-earners, since they are increasingly being replaced by robots/automation. What is more, the capital share rises, independently of the elasticity of substitution. [The modified Solow model] highlights the central distributional dilemma: that the benefits from growth now increasingly accrue through rising profits. (Atkinson & Bourguignon, 2014, p. xilx)

In line with the argument of a distribution dilemma, Roine and Waldenström (2014, p. 79)—though they are skeptical of any "mechanical relationship between inequality and industrialization or technological change"—argue that: "the technological development starting in the 1970s constitute[s] the start of a shift, not from agriculture to industry as in Kuznets' original story, but from traditional industry to an ICT-intensive sector that initially rewards a small part of the population, but eventually will spread, bringing inequality down."[1]

There is thus a theoretical case that automation may be linked to income inequality and wage stagnation. Is there also a case for it leading to technological unemployment? The Solow model and its iterations suggest greater output (i.e. supply) due to automation which should translate into lower prices under conditions of competition. Lower prices in turn should lead to greater quantities demanded which necessitate more net employment of humans.

So, the net effect of using labor-saving technology could still be labor-increasing domestically. It may, however, not be if we took the Summers' model to its extreme: this would mean assuming a *perfectly* labor-saving production function where labor drops out entirely as a factor of production. In that case, output would be produced solely by nonhuman production factors.

Solow himself was skeptical of such a scenario. In a book on unemployment in the United States written in the 1960s, he noted that "rather spectacular scientific and engineering achievements" have led many "to the conclusion that there is a kind of revolution in progress, connected with the advance of automation" (Solow, 1964, p. 7). Yet, he doubted "that the clichés about automation and structural unemployment are very productive in analyzing the problem or bringing the remedy any closer" (ibid., p. 40) and he was particularly skeptical that automation calls for specific policy responses or a reorganization of the economic framework.

Of course, as noted above, not all labor is equally easy to substitute with machines. The dominant view has been that technology is skills-complementing or skills-biased (see Tinbergen, 1974, 1975). Empirically, models predicting a "skills premium" and rising market inequality due to automation are pervasive (see Acemoglu & Autor, 2011; Autor, Katz, & Kearney, 2004; Goldin & Katz, 2007; Katz & Autor, 1999; Katz & Murphy, 2013). Others have argued, though, that technological change does not *necessarily* have to be skills-biased and inequality-increasing in every case (see Roine & Waldenström, 2014).

The neoclassical growth model is a one-sector model and thus indifferent to the role of structural change in driving growth as Lewis (1954) intended, in his vision of economic development as a transfer of labor from a low-productivity, "traditional" sector to a higher productivity, "modern" sector. Herrendorf, Rogerson, and Valentinyi (2014) argue empirically that the sectoral composition of economic activity is key to understanding economic development. McMillan and Rodrik (2011, p. 1), also, in taking sectoral and aggregate labor productivity data empirically show that the transfer of labor and other inputs to higher productive activity is a driver of economic development, as Lewis hypothesized. However, they go on to note that structural change can in fact be growth-enhancing *or* growth-reducing, depending on the reallocation of that labor.[2] Assuming technological labor-substitution, what can we say about potential implications for structural economic transformation, i.e. the reallocation of economic resources across sectors with different levels of productivity?

The dual economy model of Lewis (1954) is based, as noted, on a traditional or subsistence sector and a modern sector, where in the former, there is a surplus of unproductive labor that is sustained by receiving an equal share of the total product for reasons of traditional/family-based values. Lewis argued that the driver of economic development was a sectoral movement of labor from the "traditional" or "subsistence" or "non-capitalist" sector (of low productivity, low wage, priced to average product not marginal product, and thus widespread disguised unemployment) to the "modern" or "capitalist" sector (of higher productivity, and where wages are set by productivity in the "subsistence sector."

A critical factor is the existence of surplus labor in the traditional sector. Because of this, wages are set just above subsistence across the whole economy, leading to the transfer of labor over time from the traditional to the modern sector, and the capture of labor productivity gains to capitalists as profits, as these are the source of growth via reinvestment. The floor for wages is institutionally set at subsistence. When surplus labor disappears, an integrated labor market and economy emerge, and wages will then start to rise.

The Lewis model was intended as a critique of the neoclassical approach in that labor is available to the modern or capitalist sector of an economy not in a perfectly elastic supply but upward sloping rather than flat, and with a distinction between surplus-producing labor and subsistence labor (the latter of which was a negligible source of net profits for reinvestment, which Lewis saw as the driver for growth).

Diao, McMillan, Rodrik, and Kennedy (2017, pp. 3–4) seek to link the structural dualism of Lewis with the neoclassical model, by arguing that the neoclassical model shows the growth process within the modern sector and the dual model shows the relationship between sectors. In short, the emergence of a modern sector with higher and competitively paid wages, and where profits are reinvested by capital owners, creates a pull force. This pull force attracts labor from the traditional sector. After a period of labor exchange via migration, an inter-sectoral equilibrium is reached, and wages are equalized between sectors.

Following Lewis' dual economy, we could divide up an economy into two sectors: an *automation-prone sector* (APS), consisting of jobs that are easy to perform by machines, and an *automation-resistant sector* (ARS), consisting of jobs that are hard to perform by machines (Fig. 5.1).[3] The former would, for instance, include simple manual routine tasks like

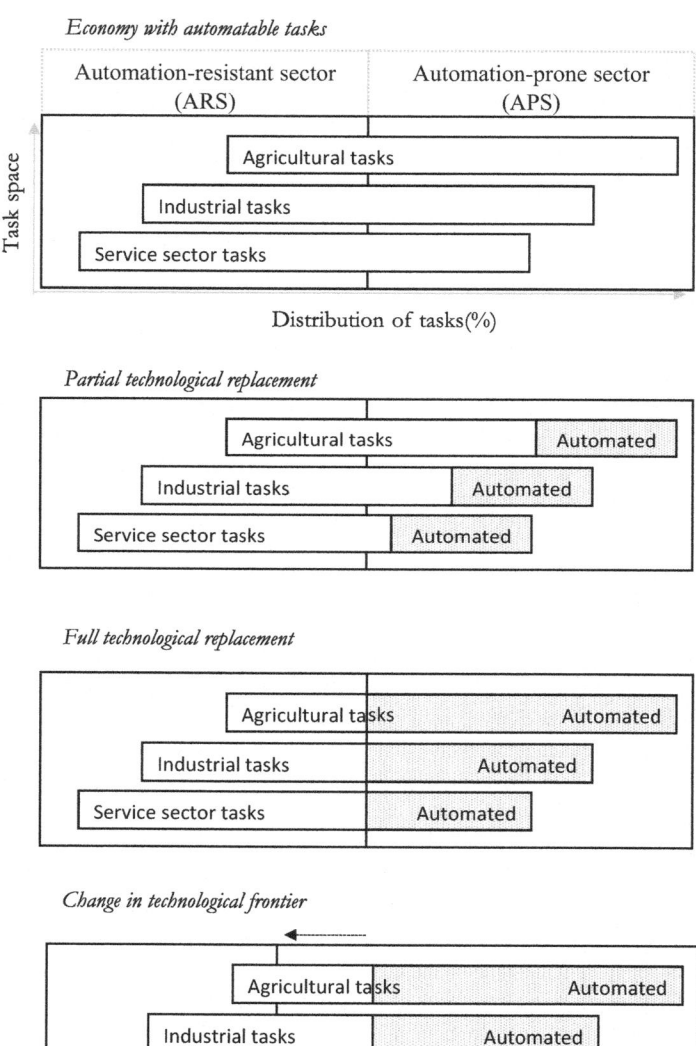

Fig. 5.1 Structural change in a "dual economy" defined by automatability. *Source* Authors' imagination

lifting, drilling, and so forth and the latter would, for instance, include creative work involving face-to-face interaction.

With a view to the Lewis model of economic development, one could say that automation creates "unlimited supplies of artificial labor" in the APS. The increasing use of robots is thus equivalent to labor force growth in the APS. Arguably, the sheer capacity alone to build and deploy robots creates a new kind of "robot reserve army" in the APS, limiting the bargaining power and wages of labor in that sector. If automation is (technologically, legally, politically, and socially) feasible, the labor force will thus gradually be pushed from the APS into the ARS. There would be automation-driven structural change taking place.

In other words, automation itself constitutes a supply shock which shifts the labor supply curve in the APS to the right, and thus reduces the equilibrium wage in that sector (as well as in the ARS to the extent that labor can be absorbed in that sector). If the unit cost of automated production falls below the reservation wage of workers, a labor surplus is created. Automation thus frees up resources for the completion of non-automatable work.[4] The surplus can either be absorbed by the ARS or, in case that is not possible, can lead to technological unemployment. Like in the Lewis model, the functional distribution of income changes in favor of capital owners.

Is there a "turning point"? In Lewis' standard model, a turning point is reached when surplus labor has fully migrated from the traditional or subsistence sector to the modern industrial sector, and wages start rising in the traditional sector due to an emerging labor shortage. In the model outlined here, there is, arguably, no such turning point. The supply of "artificial labor," i.e. automation, is genuinely unlimited, as it does not depend on demographic growth. In that case, human labor in the APS is fully displaced by machines and only an ARS remains. The ARS is itself, of course, not static but is defined by the technological frontier of the time. Technological innovation then gives rise to the shift of the frontier and thus reemergence of a new APS.

The question then becomes: What industries and tasks comprise the ARS and the APS, respectively? And is demand for the ARS large enough to allow full employment at decent wages? Regarding the first question, it would arguably be a mistake to suspect the location of the ARS primarily in newly emerging post-industrial sectors such as telecommunication or finance. Rather, the little amount of human work performed in modern agriculture is equally as automation-resistant by today's technological standards as resilient jobs in the industrial and the service sectors.[5] The service sector is generally considered to contribute strongly to the ARS, as it involves plenty of nonroutine work involving social interactions. The current occupational structure of an economy reflects past (expectations of) automatability.

Regarding the second question, there could be a dilemma whereby a productivity boost in the APS (e.g. in agriculture) creates surplus labor, but the ARS (e.g. the industrial sector) is not able to fully absorb it. So-called premature deindustrialization could be due to such "Lewis 2.0" dynamics: workers might be moving to the service sector because the manufacturing sector has no demand for (unskilled) labor. It is fully imaginable from today's point of view that the industrial sector will at some point be absorbing an equally small number of workers as today's extractive and agricultural sectors are. A set of highly productive manufacturing clusters would then produce most of the physical goods there is demand for, while almost all human labor demand would remain in the service sector.

If that is the case, this would indicate that the digital revolution creates problems for analysis based on broad economic sectors such as "services": Castells (2010, p. 244) criticizes analysis based on sectors for three flaws: (i) the extreme heterogeneity of the service sector creates a "statistically obsolete category" which (ii) underestimates the "revolutionary nature of new information technologies" and (iii) the diversity of advanced societies and interdependence with the global economy from which different employment and occupational structures follow.

The historical productivity revolution in agriculture (or the "Green Revolution" in developing countries) shows how transformative and labor-saving technological change can be. In the British census of 1841, 22% of citizens were registered as being in agricultural employment whereas this number has dropped to below 1% in the present (Office for National Statistics, 2013). Agricultural shares in the developing world, though considerably higher, have also fallen rapidly (to an extent that Eastwood, Kirsten, & Lipton [2007] have argued that developing countries underwent "premature agriculturalization").

Green revolutions have brought drastic productivity gains, allowing and incentivizing the reallocation of labor toward other—often hitherto nonexistent—economic activities and sectors. Many argue that technological leaps in agriculture allowed Western countries to escape a

"Malthusian trap" which had kept living standards stagnant throughout most of preindustrial history (see Clark, 2008). Had there been policies to prevent the agricultural revolution because of job losses, the industrial revolution may not have unfolded in the same way. Historical structural change thus holds lessons, both for how hitherto unknown sectors can absorb labor from shrinking sectors, and what potential risks are involved in counteracting structural change.

The Industrial Revolution provides another point of reference for the digital transformation. Avent (2017, p. 162) argues that the digital revolution is set to repeat the experience of the Industrial Revolution which "bypassed the developing world for long decades." In Avent's view, integration into global supply chains which enabled rapid catch-up growth in the South ("export-led industrialization") was a transitory phenomenon that will soon be replaced by both "reshoring"—the repatriation of outsourced production—or will be limited to small high-tech clusters in developing economies (cf. Yusuf, 2017). Such clusters might not create the large-scale job opportunities that broad-based industrial activity provided historically. According to Avent (2017, p. 163), the digital revolution will thus "make it more difficult in the future for poor countries to repeat the performance of the past twenty years. Once again, rich economies will enjoy a near-monopoly on the sorts of social capital required to generate a rich-world income" such as democracy, property rights, and accountable governance. One could call this the threat of a "disruption" of the catch-up development process.[6]

5.3 THE FOURTH INDUSTRIAL RESERVE ARMY

What can be said about the characteristics of a labor surplus? Lewis (1954), in his seminal text on unlimited supplies of labor, saw himself working "in the classical tradition" of Karl Marx and Adam Smith.

In *Das Kapital*, Karl Marx (2012 [1867]) posited that there is a "progressive production of a relative surplus population or Industrial Reserve Army" (ibid., p. 274) as both a condition and an outcome of the capitalist mode of production.[7] Overpopulation, in Marx' view, provides a "mass of human material always ready for exploitation" (ibid., p. 276), holding the wages of the active labor force in check and thus feeding a process of capital accumulation. Throughout this process of accumulation, the productiveness of labor constantly expands with growing employment of machinery. This accelerating capital accumulation process leads, in Marx' view, to a "constant transformation of a part of the laboring population into unemployed or half-employed hands" (ibid., p. 278), i.e. a surplus population relative to the labor demand of industry (rather than an absolute overpopulation in a Malthusian sense).

Marx had a strong interest in the relationship of technology and labor in the production process, and he specifically points to the "automatic factories" where "only a very small number continue to find employment," while the majority who get laid off form a "floating surplus population" (ibid., p. 281). He speaks of workers being degraded to the estranging status of an "appendage of a machine" (ibid.) and, in *Das Kapital*, Marx sees the process of technology-driven capitalistic development as an "accumulation of misery" (ibid.). This line of argument is stark techno-pessimism.

Although Lewis' conception of surplus labor as a population defined "relatively to capital and natural resources" sounds Marxian (and also Malthusian), there are some differences in that Lewis really means *disguised* rather than actual unemployment. In other words, Lewis' surplus population receive wages and, moreover, these wages exceed their marginal productivity (cf. Lewis, 1954, pp. 141f.).[8] Marx (2012, p. 283), on the other hand, distinguished multiple forms of surplus labor: a "floating" form where workers have to constantly change employers; a "latent" form of precarious agricultural (under)employment; a "stagnant" form characterized by irregular employment at minimal wages; and a "pauperist form" which is made up of criminals and "dangerous classes." Lewis' conception of surplus labor thus resembles that of Marx' *latent* surplus, whereas he explicitly disagrees with the notion of productivity-driven labor surplus:

"Marx offered a third source of labor to add to the reserve army, namely the unemployment generated by increasing efficiency. (…) Nowadays we reject this argument on empirical grounds. It is clear that the effect of capital accumulation in the past has been to reduce the size of the reserve army, and not to increase it, so we have lost interest in arguments about what is 'theoretically' possible" (Lewis, 1954, p. 145).

Lewis was thus a technological optimist. Indeed, if the industrialized/urban/capitalistic sector in his model is *also* assumed to produce surplus labor, the model of labor exchange would arguably break down.

Marx and Lewis concur that the reserve army is central to capital accumulation in modern capitalism. Lewis (1954, p. 145), though, is much more sanguine about this process as he sees the "expansion of new industries or new employment opportunities without any shortage of unskilled labor." When in Sect. 5.2, we proposed to understand automation along the lines of a "Lewis 2.0 model" the idea was thus to incorporate elements of both Marxian and Lewisian thinking: in light of current technological development, we may not want to reject Marx' views on automation "on empirical grounds" quite as categorically as Lewis did—even if the impact of reserve army dynamics are more likely wage pressures in the APS rather than the drastic employment-destroying effects of the "automatic factory" that Marx had in mind.

Lewis, on the other hand, may have been right in considering surplus labor primarily as an *engine of structural change* within a dualistic economy framework. Labor that is "set free" may get permanently absorbed in the ARS. The question then is whether such modern-day automation-driven structural change has equally benign effects (particularly under conditions of global competition and an international division of labor), as Lewis assumed traditional structural change to have, in labor-abundant Asian developing countries.[9]

5.4 Existing Empirical Forecasts of the Employment Effects of Automation

It is an empirical question if and in what sectors automation reduces labor demand. As was discussed, automation could reduce employment if the ARS has a low demand for labor. But if productivity gains lead to lower prices and thus higher quantities demanded, net job effects could be positive. Furthermore, the demand for new labor-intensive work could rise as the cost of labor falls relative to capital. Many would argue that the very problem of developing countries is that there is too little, rather than too much, automation and thus lower labor productivity.

Table 5.1 presents a further layer to the "Lewis 2.0" model of economic development in an analytical framework to consider automation effects on employment within the two-sector model presented earlier. One could speak of an adaptable and a non-adaptable labor force (defined, for instance, by the skills level).

One could then hypothesize the existence of two opposing forces in automation-driven structural change in the developing world: (i) labor

Table 5.1 The labor dynamics of automation in a dual economy

Technology	Labor	Response	Outcome
Complementary	Adapted	Keep/hire	Structural stability
Substitutive	Adaptable	Retrain/switch task Lower wage	Structural change
	Non-adaptable	Lay off	

Source Authors' imagination

is cheaper than in high-income countries, thus more competitive vis-à-vis machines, and there is thus less of an incentive to automate; and (ii) conversely, given widespread low-skilled manual routine work, work tasks that are prevalent in developing countries are easier to automate from a technological viewpoint. In other words, the APS will likely be larger in developing countries. Considering the taxonomy that was proposed earlier, this means that automation is arguably more technologically but less economically feasible.

Empirical estimates and forecasts of the potential impact of automation across the world are presented in Table 5.2 (the table is non-exhaustive). It is immediately evident from the studies in Table 5.2 that there is no consensus on jobs impacts and substantial variation in current estimates.

Estimates range from alarming scenarios, according to which there is a "50% chance of AI outperforming humans *in all tasks* within 45 years" (Grace, Salvatier, Dafoe, Zhang, & Evans, 2017, emphasis added), on the one hand, to contrasting claims of there being "no evidence that automation leads to joblessness" (Mishel & Bivens, 2017, p. 1), and the sarcastic recommendation that "everyone should take a deep breath" (Atkinson & Wu, 2017, p. 23).

The seminal study in the recent automation literature is that of Frey and Osborne (2013) for the United States, and subsequent studies have reproduced and refined their methodology. They conclude that almost half of the US employment is "at risk." In contrast, Arntz, Gregory, and Zierahn (2016) occupies a middle ground in terms of optimism. The authors argue with some plausibility for a "task-based" rather than an—inevitably oversimplified—"occupation-based" approach to estimating automatability risk. Arntz et al. draw on data from an international survey of adult skills conducted across OECD countries which contains data

Table 5.2 Estimates of the employment impact of automation

Authors	Region	Findings
Studies of OECD countries		
Frey and Osborne (2013)	US	"47 percent of total US employment is at risk" (ibid., p. 1)
Barany and Siegel (2014)	US	ICTs substitute middle-skill occupations
Acemoglu and Restrepo (2015)	n/a	"Automation, by reducing wages relative to the rental rate of capital, encourages the creation of new labor-intensive tasks" (ibid., p. 41)
Arntz et al. (2016)	OECD	9% of jobs automatable but "jobs at risk" may not translate into employment loss; large negative job effects "unlikely"
Bessen (2016)	US	During 1984–2007 computer use was associated with a 3% average annual job loss in manufacturing but a 1% increase elsewhere
Executive Office of the President of the United States (2016)	US	"Economy has repeatedly proven itself capable of handling this scale of change," but jobs at risk "concentrated among lower-paid, lower skilled, and less-educated workers" (ibid., p. 2)
Acemoglu and Restrepo (2017)	US	"One additional robot per thousand workers (…) reduces aggregate employment to population ratio by 0.34 percentage points and aggregate wages by 0.5 percent" (ibid., p. 36)
Atkinson and Wu (2017)	US	Labor market disruption occurring at its lowest rate since the Civil War
IMF (2017)	Advanced economies	Technological progress "explains about half the overall decline [of the labor income share] in advanced economies, with a larger negative impact on the earnings of middle-skilled workers"
Mishel and Bivens (2017)	US	No evidence that automation leads to joblessness or inequality
PWC (2017)	OECD	Automation could replace 38% jobs in the United States, 35% in Germany, 30% in the UK, and 21% in Japan by early 2030s
Studies of developing countries		
Chandy (2017)	Developing countries	"Automation is likely to replace jobs even faster in developing countries than in industrial ones" (ibid., p. 15)

(continued)

Table 5.2 (continued)

Authors	Region	Findings
Chang and Huynh (2016)	South East Asia	56% of jobs are at high risk of automation in Association of Southeast Asian Nations (ASEAN) countries
Frey et al. (2016)	Developing countries	"Developing countries are highly susceptible to the expanding scope of automation" (ibid., p. 18)
Frey and Rahbari (2016)	OECD and Ethiopia, India and China	China will lose 77% of jobs to automation, India 69%, Ethiopia 85%, and OECD average 57% jobs lost
World Bank (2016)	Developing Countries	Two-thirds of all jobs susceptible to automation (1.8 bn jobs), but the effects are moderated by lower wages and slower technology adoption
Avent (2017)	Developing Countries	"New technology seems to be making life harder for the emerging world" (ibid., p. 171)
World Economic Forum (2017)	Africa	41% of all work activities in South Africa susceptible to automation, 44% in Ethiopia, 46% in Nigeria, and 52% in Kenya
ADB (2018)	Asia	In the period of 2005–2015 in 12 Asian economies there were 101 m job losses per annum due to "modern machine tools and ICT equipment" which were offset by 134 m jobs created due to higher demand for goods and services (ibid., pp. 77–78)
Global studies		
Grace et al. (2017)	Global	50% chance of AI outperforming humans in all tasks in 45 years and of automating all human jobs in 120 years
McKinsey Global Institute (2017a)	Global	Using existing technologies, around two-thirds of occupations could have one-third of their constitutive tasks automated

Source Sources cited

on the tasks performed for each type of job. The authors use these data to impute a score of automatability, as well as the size of the population at "high risk" of automation. Interestingly, Russia's occupational structure is deemed least automatable of the 21 countries considered, whereas Germany and Austria top the rank. Put differently, the country with the lowest gross domestic product (GDP) per capita (and per worker) in the data set considered by Arntz et al. (2016) shows the highest *resilience* to automation. Generally, there is no consistent relationship with GDP per capita and their score of automatability, though, in this OECD data set (which is based on a selection of structurally similar economies).

The McKinsey Global Institute (2017b) provides estimates of employment that is susceptible to automation for 52 countries, which is the most comprehensive global data set we know of. Overall, McKinsey is considerably more pessimistic with their estimates of mean automatability, being on average 10 percentage points above that of Arntz et al. Their estimates are more pessimistic in every country and considerably more pessimistic specifically regarding non-OECD countries.[10] Across Western OECD countries only, the estimates of Arntz et al. and McKinsey are, in fact, closely aligned ($r^2 = 0.5$). Their automatability estimates of industrialized economies such as Russia, Korea, and Japan, though, differ significantly, with McKinsey being considerably more pessimistic.

Another recent global estimate comes from the World Bank (2016) who provide data for 40 countries and are yet more pessimistic, with average estimates lying 20 percentage points above the McKinsey estimate. The overlap of country coverage between the World Bank and the McKinsey estimates is small (nine countries); among those, the shared variance is relatively low at about 12% (Table 5.3 shows selected countries). In addition to automatability estimates, the World Bank also

Table 5.3 Estimates of the proportion of employment that is automatable in selected countries

	MGI (2017c) (%)	World Bank (2016) (%)
Argentina	48	65
China	51	77
Costa Rica	52	68
Ethiopia	50	85
India	52	69
Malaysia	51	68
Nigeria	46	65
South Africa	41	67
Thailand	55	72

Sources As cited

provides adjusted estimates which take into account the different speeds of technology diffusion across countries.

In the next section, we explore the McKinsey Global Institute (2017b) and World Bank (2016) data in more detail.[11]

5.5 Empirical Patterns of Automatability and Economic Development

Instead of focusing on the levels of automatability per se, which remains fairly contentious we next discuss the relationship of automatability and economic development.[12]

The first observation to make (and one that was also made by Frey, Osborne, & Holmes, 2016) is that automatability estimates show a relationship with the level of GNI per capita across countries in global comparison (Fig. 5.2). Both sets of estimates are highly significantly ($p<0.01$) negatively correlated with gross national income (GNI) per capita. Thus, the richer an economy, the less automatable the labor force. That said, McKinsey's estimates range from a minimum of 41% to a maximum of 56% and the World Bank's from 55 to 85%, so even the most resilient countries could still see significant labor market disruption.

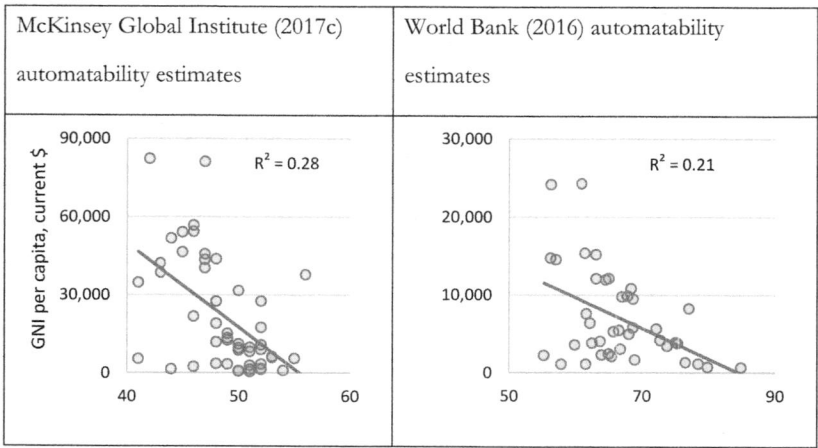

Fig. 5.2 The level of economic development and the share of employment susceptible to automation. *Source* Authors' estimates based on sources cited

It is interesting to note that the McKinsey Global Institute assigns the lowest automatability estimates to Kuwait and South Africa, the former an entirely oil-fueled Organization of the Petroleum Exporting Countries (OPEC) economy with practically no unemployment, and the latter having one of the highest unemployment rates and most segregated labor markets in the world. Overall, the median estimates of the McKinsey Global Institute for HICs ($n=27$) is 47, whereas the median for low-income countries (LICs) and lower middle-income countries (LMICs) ($n=13$) is 51.

It is worth at this point considering the structural characteristics of economies. Figure 5.3 reproduces the familiar cross-country pattern across three sectors, showing that rich countries generally have very low levels of employment in agriculture and high levels of service sector employment, with the reverse being the case for developing countries. The industry share of employment is uncorrelated with GNI per capita ($p>0.05$) from a cross-country perspective.

Given this overall structural pattern, what then is the relationship between automatability and sectoral characteristics? Figure 5.4 shows that the pattern is similar, though somewhat less pronounced, to the pattern of GNI per capita and automatability. The service sector share, in particular, is a strong predictor of both McKinsey's and the World Bank's automatability estimates. The more agrarian an economy is, the larger the population performing tasks that machines could theoretically perform.

We can thus say, assuming the automatability estimates are reasonable, that the labor force of more service sector-based, richer economies tends to be less replaceable compared to more agriculture-based, poorer economies. This pattern is intuitive and is explained by the complexity and creativity of service-sector work and the amount of face-to-face human interaction involved in it. If we break down the relationship of sectoral employment by level of GNI per capita (Fig. 5.5), the above-mentioned pattern largely holds. Among HICs, there is no relationship between agriculture and automatability simply because there is almost no employment in agriculture. Industrial work is more automatable and service-sector work less automatable across both country groupings, so the level of economic development does not moderate that sectoral relationship.[13]

Generally, we can say the APS is (much) larger in countries with lower income per capita. If countries have to decide how to reallocate employment during structural change and the described cross-country pattern

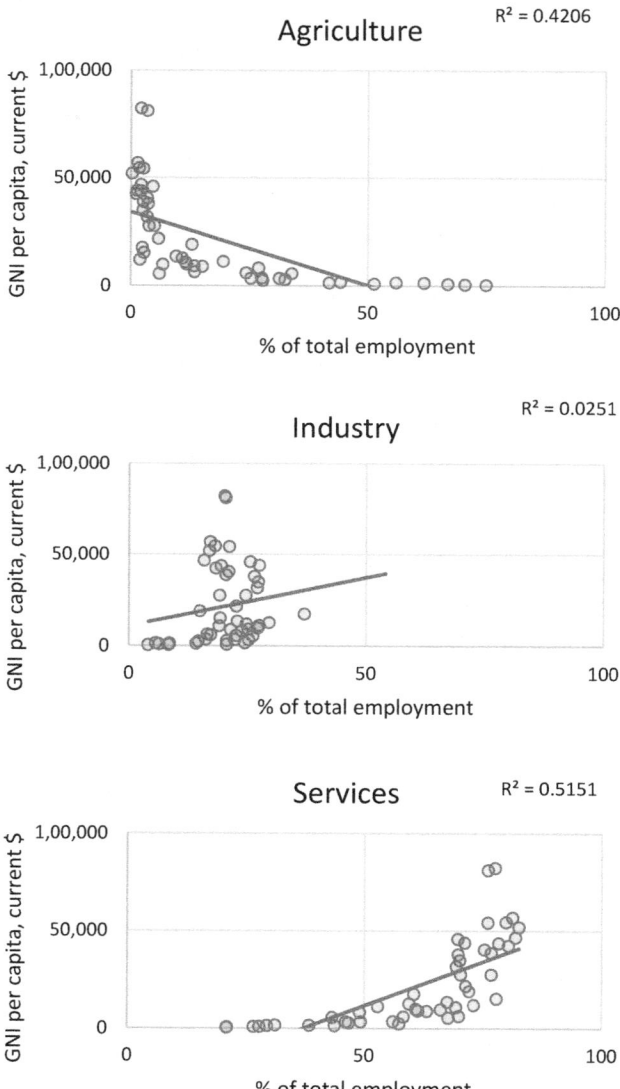

Fig. 5.3 Employment by sectors and GNI per capita (2016 or most recent data). *Source* Authors' estimates based on World Bank [2016]

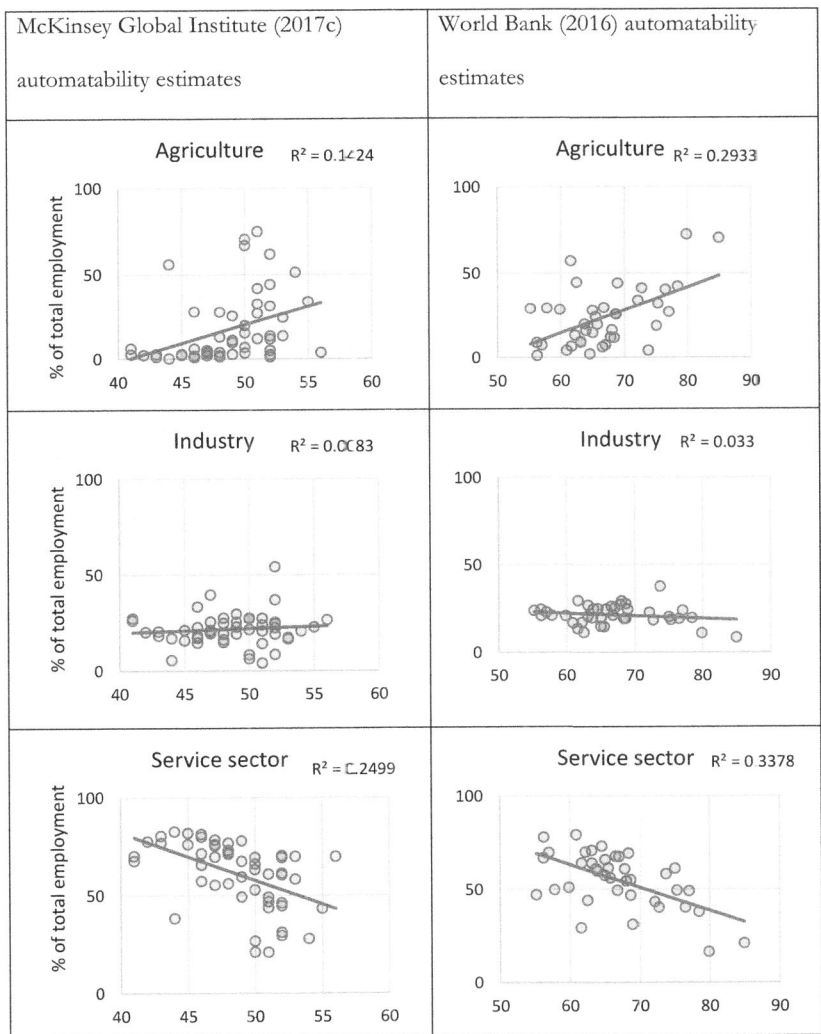

Fig. 5.4 Automatability and share of employment by sectors, 2016. *Source* Authors' estimates based on sources cited

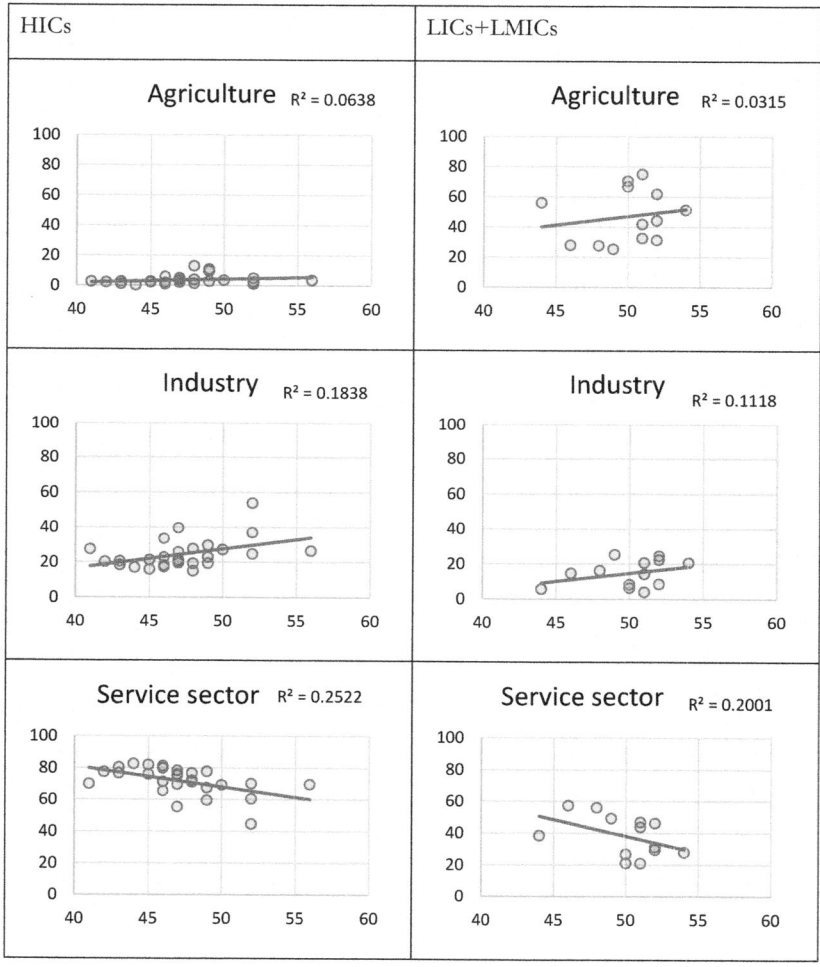

Fig. 5.5 McKinsey Global Institute's automatability estimates and employment across economic sectors by income group. *Source* Authors' calculations based on McKinsey Global Institute [2017b] and World Bank [2016]

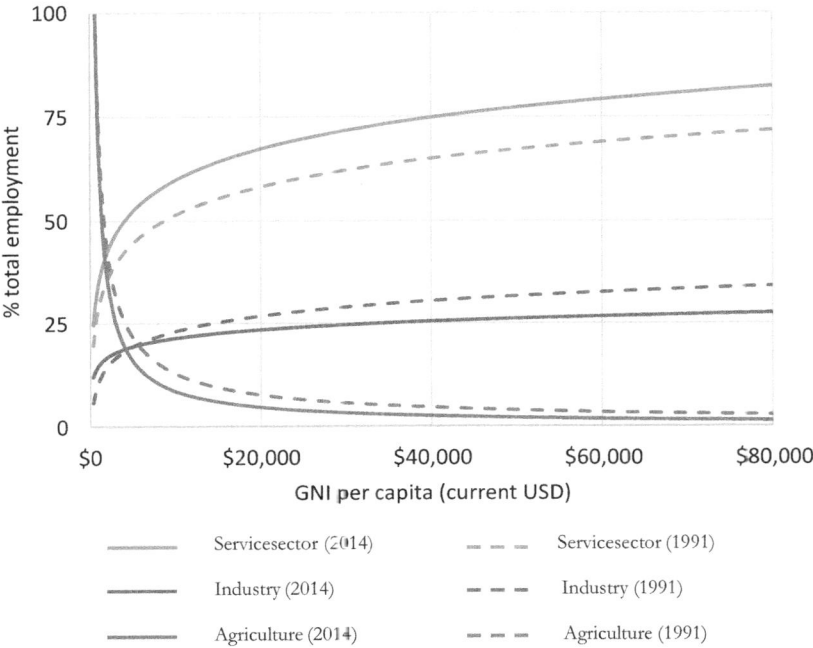

Fig. 5.6 Economic development and sectoral employment shares across countries (fitted lines): 1991 and 2014. *Source* Authors' estimates based on World Bank [2018] data

allows any inference about country-level developments over time, an increase in service-sector employment would suggest itself as the only future-proof employment growth model. In HICs, it would suggest structural change away from industrial work and in developing countries away from agriculture.

What does this mean for the future of economic development and structural transformation? Holding all else constant, sectoral differences in the replaceability of labor will sustain a pressure for both further deindustrialization and deagriculturalization. This is not a new phenomenon: in fact, the cross-country pattern of sectoral employment shares shown earlier in Fig. 5.4 and reproduced in Fig. 5.6 to compare 1991 and 2014 (fitted lines) shows a surprising degree of continuity over time. What appears to be happening, though, is an expansion of service-sector employment in the richest countries, and a reduction in the share of industrial work compared to the early nineties (this pattern is corroborated by Wood, 2017). In line with this, Chandy (2017, p. 14) speculates that "China may be one of the last countries to ride the wave of industrialization to prosperity." Generally, most of the global cross-country variability of employment shares is found toward the low end of the GNI per capita, whereas countries above a per capita GNI of 20,000 look structurally very similar, i.e. are highly service-based and thus face lower automatability. In general, it is only in the poorest countries that a considerable proportion of labor is in agriculture. However, even in middle-income developing countries such as Indonesia and Thailand, a third of the labor force remains in agriculture. Agriculture employs only a few percent of labor force in wealthy countries. This suggests that in contrast to OECD countries, many jobs in developing countries have likely been automatable for a long time.

Notes

1. Roine and Waldenström (2014) suggest a new Kuznets curve based on technological developments starting not a sectoral shift of agriculture to industry but a shift from traditional industry to technologically intensive industry. If a given technology makes skilled workers more productive and there is an increase in the relative demand for those workers, the rewards accrue to a small proportion of the population who are skilled workers. Based on Tinbergen's (1974, 1975) hypothesis that the returns to skills are a competition between education and technology, the supply of skilled workers then determines whether or not their wages rise. Roine and Waldenström argue that the drivers of the Kuznets downturn are political and exogenous shocks.
2. McMillan and Rodrik show how structural change had been growth-enhancing in Asia because labor has transferred from low to higher productivity sectors. However, the converse is the case for sub-Saharan Africa and Latin America because labor has been transferred from higher to lower productivity sectors and this has reduced growth rates. They find that countries with a large share of exports in natural resources tend to experience growth-reducing structural transformation and, even if they have higher productivity, cannot absorb surplus labor from agriculture.

3. This of course has resonance with Baumol (1967) who in a similar fashion divided up the economy into "technologically progressive" and "technologically non-progressive" activities. In the former, productivity-driving, sector "labor is primarily an instrument (…) while in other (…) labor is itself the end product" (ibid., p. 416). One issue is our approach implies a somewhat linear view of structural change that does not take into account the servicification of manufacturing and therefore an overlap between APS and ARS. This would also mean for Table 5.1 that even complementarity could drive structural change in that the services that digitization adds to manufacturing could drive industrialization.
4. Baumol's "unbalanced growth" model similarly envisaged a labor transition from one to the other sector and aggregate stagnant labor productivity as a result (Baumol, 1967; Baumol, Blackman, & Wolff, 1985; see also Ngai & Pissarides, 2017 for a contemporary iteration of the model). Autor and Dorn (2013), based on a spatial equilibrium model, posit a reallocation of low-skill labor into service occupations (a phenomenon they call "employment polarization" which then entails wage polarization).
5. Of course, both the existence of agricultural subsidies and trade of agricultural products makes an assessment more difficult. Without subsidies, the sector might employ even fewer people. Conversely, OECD countries are not self-sufficient and depend on labor in foreign countries to produce food for export to OECD countries.
6. The concept of disruption or disruptive innovation goes back to Christensen's (1997) book *The Innovator's Dilemma*. In it, he describes how emerging technologies developed by small challengers can threaten dominant and generally well-managed businesses. Disruption generally means an unanticipated, revolutionary transformation that impacts an established market. Such disruption could happen to global value chains and thus the export-oriented industrialization development model.
7. One issue Marx would have raised is the ownership of the intellectual property that drives robots, and the reinvestment of related rents.
8. For Lewis, wages are set at subsistence level, but since the marginal productivity of surplus workers is assumed to be (close to) zero, *any* wage they get exceeds their marginal contribution: "…large sectors of the economy where the marginal productivity of labor is negligible, zero, or even negative"—i.e. the subsistence sectors (1954, p. 141). And wage earners in that case receive "wages exceeding marginal productivity" (ibid.). The implication is that one can pull out workers from that sector without reducing the total output of the sector (or even increasing it in case of negative marginal productivity).

9. Lewis believed in contrast to Asia that Africa had a labor shortage due to agricultural land availability. The constraint to growth in Africa was low agriculture productivity rather than manufacturing growth and required government intervention in agriculture (See Kanbur, 2016, p. 7).
10. A second MGI report (MGI, 2017b) released later the same year was much less pessimistic. It estimated labor displacement at 400 m jobs globally which would be offset by 555 million jobs created by increased labor demand.
11. There are further data sets of IMF (2017) and UNCTAD (2017) which we do not have access to at time of writing.
12. We may overemphasize the technical feasibility angle in this section given the data we use which leads us to an inverse relationship between automatability and per capita income. At the current cost of automation, there is a positive relationship and the curve may turn into an inverted U as costs keeps falling and all jobs in developed countries have been automated, before eventually becoming negative; the question of course is how long away "eventually" is. Thus our assessment may be too pessimistic.
13. There is a significant ($p<0.05$) positive correlation of industrial employment shares and automatability in HICs. This pattern is also found using the data of Arntz et al. (2016). It can similarly be observed in developing countries (non-HICs) in the McKinsey Global Institute (2017b) data where it is though not significant as data coverage is too limited.

References

Acemoglu, D., & Autor, D. (2011). Skills, tasks and technologies: Implications for employment and earnings. In O. Ashenfelter & D. Card (Eds.), *Handbook of labor economics* (Vol. 4B, pp. 1043–1171). Amsterdam: Elsevier.

Acemoglu, D., & Restrepo, P. (2015). The race between machine and man: Implications of technology for growth, factor shares and employment. *SSRN Electronic Journal*. https://doi.org/10.2139/ssrn.2781320.

Acemoglu, D., & Restrepo, P. (2017). *Robots and jobs: Evidence from US labor markets* (NBER Working Paper Series No. 23285). Cambridge, MA: NBER. Retrieved from http://www.nber.org/papers/w23285.

ADB (Asian Development Bank). (2018). *Asian development outlook 2018: How technology affects jobs*. Manila: ADB.

Arntz, M., Gregory, T., & Zierahn, U. (2016). The risk of automation for jobs in OECD countries: A comparative analysis. *OECD Social, Employment and Migration Working Papers, 2*(189), 47–54.

Atkinson, A. B., & Bourguignon, F. (2014). Introduction: Income distribution today. In A. B. Atkinson & F. Bourguignon (Eds.), *Handbook of income distribution, volume 2A* (pp. xvii–lxiv). Oxford and Amsterdam: Elsevier.

Atkinson, R. D., & Wu, J. (2017). *False alarmism: Technological disruption and the U.S. labor market, 1850–2015*. @Work Series. Retrieved from http://www2.itif.org/2017-false-alarmism-technological-disruption.pdf.

Autor, D. H., & Dorn, D. (2013). The growth of low-skill service jobs and the polarization of the US labor market. *American Economic Review, 103*(5), 1553–1597.

Autor, D. H., Katz, L. F., & Kearney, M. S. (2004). The polarization of the U.S. labor market. *AEA Papers and Proceedings, 96*(2), 189–194.

Avent, R. (2017). *The wealth of humans: Work and its absence in the twenty-first century*. London: Penguin Random House.

Barany, Z., & Siegel, C. (2014). *Job polarization and structural change*. Retrieved from https://www.aeaweb.org/conference/2015/retrieve.php?pdfid=237.

Baumol, W. J. (1967). Macroeconomics of unbalanced growth: The anatomy of urban crisis. *The American Economic Review, 57*(3), 415–426.

Baumol, W. J., Blackman, B., & Wolff, E. N. (1985). Unbalanced growth revisited: Asymptotic stagnancy and new evidence. *The American Economic Review, 75*(4), 806–817.

Bessen, J. (2016). *How computer automation affects occupations: Technology, jobs, and skills* (Law & Economics Working Paper No. 15–49). Boston, MA. Retrieved from https://papers.ssrn.com/sol3/papers.cfm?abstract_id=2690435.

Castells, M. (2010). *The rise of the network society: The information age: Economy, society, and culture*. Hoboken, NJ: Wiley Blackwell.

Chandy, L. (2017). *The future of work in the developing world: Brookings Blum roundtable 2016 post-conference report*. Washington, DC: Brookings Institution.

Chang, J.-H., & Huynh, P. (2016). *ASEAN in transformation: The future of jobs at risk of automation* (Bureau for Employers' Activities Working Paper No. 9). Bangkok. Retrieved from http://www.ilo.org/wcmsp5/groups/public/—ed_dialogue/—act_emp/documents/publication/wcms_579554.pdf.

Christensen, C. (1997). *The innovator's dilemma: When new technologies cause great firms to fail*. Boston, MA: Harvard Business Review Press.

Clark, G. (2008). *A farewell to alms: A brief economic history of the world*. Princeton, NJ and Oxford: Princeton University Press.

Diao, X., McMillan, M., Rodrik, D., & Kennedy, J. F. (2017). *The recent growth boom in developing economies: A structural-change perspective* (NBER Working Paper Series No. 23132). Cambridge, MA: NBER. Retrieved from http://www.nber.org/papers/w23132.

Eastwood, R., Kirsten, J., & Lipton, M. (2007). Premature deagriculturalisation? Land inequality and rural dependency in Limpopo province, South Africa. *The Journal of Development Studies, 42*(8), 1325–1349.

Executive Office of the President of the United States. (2016). *Preparing for the future of artificial intelligence*. Washington, DC Retrieved from https://obamawhitehouse.archives.gov/sites/default/files/whitehouse_files/microsites/ostp/NSTC/preparing_for_the_future_of_ai.pdf.

Frey, C. B., & Osborne, M. A. (2013). *The future of employment: How susceptible are jobs to computerisation?* Oxford Martin School, University of Oxford Working Paper. University of Oxford, UK. Retrieved from https://www.oxfordmartin.ox.ac.uk/downloads/academic/future-of-employment.pdf.

Frey, C. B., Osborne, M. A., & Holmes, C. (2016). *Technology at work v2.0: The future is not what it used to be* (Citi GPS: Global Perspectives & Solutions). Oxford. Retrieved from http://www.oxfordmartin.ox.ac.uk/downloads/reports/Citi_GPS_Technology_Work_2.pdf.

Frey, C. B., & Rahbari, E. 2016. *Do labor-saving technologies spell the death of jobs in the developing world* (Paper prepared for the 2016 Brookings Blum Roundtable).

Goldin, C., & Katz, L. F. (2007). *The race between education and technology: The evolution of U.S. educational wage differentials, 1890 to 2005* (NBER Working Paper Series No. 12984). Cambridge, MA: NBER. Retrieved from http://www.nber.org/papers/w12984.

Grace, K., Salvatier, J., Dafoe, A., Zhang, B., & Evans, O. (2017). *When will AI exceed human performance? Evidence from AI experts* (arXiv No. 1705.08807v2). Retrieved from http://arxiv.org/abs/1705.08807.

Herrendorf, B., Rogerson, R., & Valentinyi, A. (2014). *Growth and structural transformation* (NBER Working Paper Series No. 18996). Cambridge, MA: NBER. Retrieved from http://www.nber.org/papers/w18996.

IMF. (2017). *World economic outlook, April 2017: Gaining momentum?* Washington, DC: IMF. Retrieved from http://www.imf.org/en/Publications/WEO/Issues/2017/04/04/world-economic-outlook-april-2017.

Kanbur, R. (2016). *W. Arthur Lewis and the Roots of Ghanaian Economic Policy* (Working Paper). Charles H. Dyson School of Applied Economics and Management Cornell University, Ithaca, New York.

Katz, L. F., & Autor, D. H. (1999). Changes in the wage structure and earnings inequality. In O. Ashenfeher & D. Card (Eds.), *Handbook of labor economics* (Vol. 3, pp. 1463–1555). Amsterdam: Elsevier.

Katz, L. F., & Murphy, K. M. (2013). Changes in relative wages, 1963–1987: Supply and demand factors. *The Quarterly Journal of Economics, 107*(1), 35–78.

Lewis, W. A. (1954). Economic development with unlimited supplies of labour. *The Manchester School of Economic and Social Studies, 22*(2), 139–191.

Marx, K. (2012 [1867]). *Das Kapital: A critique of political economy*. Washington, DC: Regnery Publishing.

McKinsey Global Institute. (2017a). *A future that works: Automation, employment, and productivity*. Retrieved from https://www.mckinsey.com/~/media/McKinsey/Global%20Themes/Digital%20Disruption/Harnessing%20automation%20for%20a%20future%20that%20works/MGI-A-future-that-works_Full-report.ashx.

McKinsey Global Institute. (2017b). *Jobs lost, jobs gained: Workforce transitions in a time of automation*. Retrieved from https://www.mckinsey.com/~/media/McKinsey/Global%20Themes/Future%20of%20Organizations/What%20the%20future%20of%20work%20will%20mean%20for%20jobs%20skills%20and%20wages/MGI-Jobs-Lost-Jobs-Gained-Report-December-6-2017.ashx.

McKinsey Global Institute. (2017c). *Where machines could replace humans—And where they can't (yet)*. Retrieved from https://public.tableau.com/en-us/s/gallery/where-machines-could-replace-humans.

McMillan, M. S., & Rodrik, D. (2011). *Globalization, structural change and productivity growth* (NBER Working Paper Series No. 17143). Cambridge, MA: NBER. Retrieved from http://www.nber.org/papers/w17143.

Mishel, L., & Bivens, J. (2017) *The zombie robot argument lurches on: There is no evidence that automation leads to joblessness or inequality*. Washington, DC: Economic Policy Institute. Retrieved from http://www.epi.org/files/pdf/126750.pdf.

Ngai, L. R., & Pissarides, C. A. (2017). Structural change in a multi-sector model of growth. *American Economic Review, 97*(1), 429–443.

Office for National Statistics. (2013). *170 years of industrial change across England and Wales*. Retrieved from http://webarchive.nationalarchives.gov.uk/20160106001413/http://www.ons.gov.uk/ons/rel/census/2011-census-analysis/170-years-of-industry/170-years-of-industrial-changecomponent.html.

PWC (PricewaterhouseCoopers). (2017). UK Economic Outlook.

Roine, J., & Waldenström, D. (2014). *Long-run trends in the distribution of income and wealth* (IZA Discussion Paper No. 8157). Bonn: IZA. Retrieved from ftp.iza.org/dp8157.pdf.

Solow, R. M. (1956). A contribution to the theory of economic growth. *The Quarterly Journal of Economics, 70*(1), 65–94.

Solow, R. M. (1964). *The nature and sources of unemployment in the United States*. Stockholm: Almqvist and Wicksell.

Summers, L. H. (2013). Economic possibilities for our children: The 2013 Martin Feldstein lecture. *NBER Reporter, 4*, 4–6. Retrieved from http://www.nber.org/reporter/2013number4/2013no4.pdf.

Tinbergen, J. (1974). Substitution of graduate by other labour. *Kyklos, 27*(2), 217–226.

Tinbergen, J. (1975). Substitution of academically trained by other manpower. *Review of World Economics, 111*(3), 466–476.

UNCTAD. (2017). *Trade and development report 2017—Beyond austerity: Towards a global new deal*. New York and Geneva: UNCTAD.

Wood, A. (2017). *Variation in structural change around the world, 1985–2015: Patterns, causes, and implications* (UNU-WIDER Working Paper). UNU-WIDER: Helsinki. Retrieved from https://www.wider.unu.edu/sites/default/files/wp2017-34.pdf.

World Bank. (2016). *World development report: Digital dividends.* Washington, DC: World Bank.

World Bank. (2018). *World development indicators.* Retrieved from data.worldbank.org/data-catalog/world-development-indicators.

World Economic Forum. (2017). *The future of jobs and skills in the Middle East and North Africa: Preparing the region for the fourth industrial revolution* (Executive Briefing). Geneva: WEF.

Yusuf, S. (2017). Automation, AI, and the emerging economies. *Center for Global Development Blog.* Retrieved May 25, 2018, from https://www.cgdev.org/publication/automation-ai-and-emerging-economies.

Open Access This chapter is licensed under the terms of the Creative Commons Attribution 4.0 International License (http://creativecommons.org/licenses/by/4.0/), which permits use, sharing, adaptation, distribution and reproduction in any medium or format, as long as you give appropriate credit to the original author(s) and the source, provide a link to the Creative Commons license and indicate if changes were made.

The images or other third party material in this chapter are included in the chapter's Creative Commons license, unless indicated otherwise in a credit line to the material. If material is not included in the chapter's Creative Commons license and your intended use is not permitted by statutory regulation or exceeds the permitted use, you will need to obtain permission directly from the copyright holder.

CHAPTER 6

Automation, Politics, and Public Policy

Abstract Developing countries face several policy challenges unleashed by automation. Given the pace of technological change, upskilling strategies are likely not to be a panacea. Safety nets and wage subsidies may be desirable, but the question remains how to finance them (without making labor more costly and thus exacerbating a trend toward replacement). Investing in labor-heavy sectors such as infrastructure construction, social, education or healthcare provision may be a way for developing countries to manage disruptive impacts of automation though these would imply major public investments and do not in themselves substitute for a long-run strategy for economic development.

Keywords Public policy · Global universal basic income · Upskilling · Globalization · Policy space · Coping or containment

6.1 Politics and Technology

The discussion thus far points toward the potential for major shifts in employment due to automation. This process will likely have sociopolitical consequences. Macroeconomic and labor market dynamics determine the quality, quantity, and distribution of citizens' employment opportunities and thus of their wages, living standards, and class status. Such socioeconomic characteristics in turn have a profound bearing on sentiments of (in)security, relative deprivation, and societal equity which can influence political preferences and ultimately political outcomes. There is a large body of literature providing evidence for a causal relationship of this sort (see e.g. for the impact on electoral politics: Anderson, 2000; Lewis-Beck & Stegmaier, 2000; for the impact on political preferences: Finseraas, 2009; Mughan, 2018; see also the substantial literature on economic and class voting, as well as the literature on economic modernization and political values, e.g. Inglehart & Welzel, 2005).

The wider interest in the role of work and (un)employment as underpinnings of political agency goes back to early empirical social research (e.g. Jahoda, Lazarsfeld, & Zeisel, 1933), and even to the classical social theory of Karl Marx and Max Weber. As technological change influences labor market dynamics, an important field of research is the examination of modernization losers as political catalysts: specifically, so-called "technological anxiety" and resistance to innovation (see Mokyr, 1998; Mokyr, Vickers, & Ziebarth, 2015); the relationship of economic inequality, and political polarization and extremism (see Pontusson & Rueda, 2008); and the political implications of deindustrialization (see Iversen & Cusack, 2000).

6.2 Characterizing Public Policy Responses

Major political implications imply public policy responses. One can characterize policy responses to automation (Table 6.1). First, there is a class of policies that try to attenuate or reverse the automation trend. Among those, there are "quasi-Luddite" measures such as taxes and regulation that make domestic automation more (or even prohibitively) costly. Countries could also follow a strategy of what one could call "robot-substituting industrialization" where they impose tariffs on inputs/imports with nonhuman-produced contents. The problem with such strategies is that protectionism of labor is difficult to implement in an open economy. Luddite policies tend to be in conflict with integration into a globalized competitive market, as they assume that the economy can somehow be insulated from competition with automated production elsewhere. The mirror image of making automation costlier would be to reduce the costs of labor, e.g. by reducing income taxes or social insurance contributions, by reducing minimum wages, or costly labor regulations. The question is how desirable and politically feasible such strategies are.

Table 6.1 The space of potential public policy responses to automation

	Coping	Containment
Managing structural change	*Adaptability of labor* • Skills upgrading *Employment generation* • Post-industrialization/ARS • Investment in labor-intensive sectors • Public works programs • Active labor market policies	*Labor costs and regulation* • Tax cuts on labor • Wage subsidies • Lower minimum wage *Employment protection* • Job protection legislation *Automation costs and regulation* • Taxes on automation • Regulation that complicates automation • Tariffs on imports of non-primary goods
Managing inclusivity	*Unemployment protection* • Transition support • Unemployment insurance • Universal basic income	

Source Authors' elaboration

Second, there is a class of "coping strategies" for the trend toward automation. The most prominent one is to develop the skills of the labor force and (re)train workers in the APS. A widespread policy recommendation is to invest in skills and thus move the labor force away from automatable routine tasks. The problem with this approach is that (i) it is not clear what skills will be automation-resistant for a sufficient time to make the skills investment worthwhile and (ii) whether upskilling is at all realistic given the required time and monetary investment. Competition with currently available technology increasingly seems to require a tertiary education which is still very rare throughout the developing world. Given that even advanced industrialized countries are struggling to keep their labor forces competitive, the success of a skills development strategy alone remains questionable.

A second coping strategy would be to provide economic transition support as well as safety nets, unemployment insurance, or wage subsidies. This approach addresses the distributional skew which automation may create. However, such transfers presuppose the existence of a productive ARS in the first place, from which profits can be siphoned off for redistribution. In the absence of the existence of such a sector, there may be a case for the provision of international aid to support basic income guarantees or automation adjustment assistance overseas.

In many countries, one could say that the coping strategy adopted so far has been to invest in currently labor-intensive sectors such as infrastructure and construction. A—risky but potentially inevitable—long-term coping strategy for developing countries would be to anticipate automation trends and to try to (further) develop a productive post-industrial sector. If industrialization begins to look increasingly unattractive as a job creation strategy due to reshoring of hitherto outsourced production in value chains, countries would be well advised not to invest in the costly creation of manufacturing clusters but rather in the growth of a long-term ARS. Such an ARS could, for example, involve the social, education and healthcare sectors, and some forms of tourism, and infrastructure construction which are generally considered resilient despite increasing service automation. The problem with such an approach is that highly productive and tradeable services are skills-intensive, and non-tradable services (such as social care, personal services, etc.) are not (yet) highly value-adding, may not be sufficiently scalable, and may generally be too heterogenous to be targeted by post-industrial policies, in a similar way that industrial policies targeted the emergence of industrial clusters.

References

Anderson, C. J. (2000). Economic voting and political context: A comparative perspective. *Electoral Studies, 19*(2–3), 151–170.

Finseraas, H. (2009). Income inequality and demand for redistribution: A multilevel analysis of European public opinion. *Scandinavian Political Studies, 32*(1), 94–119.

Inglehart, R., & Welzel, C. (2005). *Modernization, cultural change, and democracy: The human development sequence.* Cambridge and New York, NY: Cambridge University Press.

Iversen, T., & Cusack, T. R. (2000). The causes of welfare state expansion: Deindustrialization or globalization. *World Politics, 52*(3), 313–349.

Jahoda, M., Lazarsfeld, P. F., & Zeisel, H. (1933). *Marienthal: The sociography of an unemployed community.* Leipzig: Hirzel Verlag.

Lewis-Beck, M. S., & Stegmaier, M. (2000). Economic determinants of electoral outcomes. *Annual Review of Political Science, 3,* 183–219.

Mokyr, J. (1998). The political economy of technological change: Resistance and innovation in economic history. In M. Berg & K. Bruland (Eds.), *Technological revolutions in Europe* (pp. 39–64). Cheltenham: Edward Elgar Publishers.

Mokyr, J., Vickers, C., & Ziebarth, N. L. (2015). The history of technological anxiety and the future of economic growth: Is this time different? *Journal of Economic Perspectives, 29*(3), 31–50.

Mughan, A. (2018). Economic insecurity and welfare preferences: A micro-level analysis. *Comparative Politics, 39*(3), 293–310. Retrieved from http://www.jstor.org/stable/20434042.

Pontusson, J., & Rueda, D. (2008). Inequality as a source of political polarization: A comparative analysis of twelve OECD countries. In P. Beramendi & C. Anderson (Eds.), *Democracy, inequality, and representation: A comparative perspective* (pp. 312–353). New York: Russell Sage Foundation.

Open Access This chapter is licensed under the terms of the Creative Commons Attribution 4.0 International License (http://creativecommons.org/licenses/by/4.0/), which permits use, sharing, adaptation, distribution and reproduction in any medium or format, as long as you give appropriate credit to the original author(s) and the source, provide a link to the Creative Commons license and indicate if changes were made.

The images or other third party material in this chapter are included in the chapter's Creative Commons license, unless indicated otherwise in a credit line to the material. If material is not included in the chapter's Creative Commons license and your intended use is not permitted by statutory regulation or exceeds the permitted use, you will need to obtain permission directly from the copyright holder.

CHAPTER 7

Conclusions

Abstract In this chapter, we conclude and identify areas for future research. We stress three points. First, automation is challenging any competitive advantage of low-cost labor of late developers. Second, due to low levels of skills, the labor force in many developing countries is vulnerable to replacement by labor-saving technology. Wage stagnation and premature deindustrialization are already unfolding—however, unemployment is not (yet) the main problem of technological change. Third, we need to ask different policy and research questions and be concerned about the jobs impact of technology and the political economy of automation rather than just automatability in principle. In that vein, the Lewis model and surplus labor theory could once more help us understand the dynamics of economic development and structural transformation.

Keywords Public policy · Reserve army · Labor surplus · Disruption · Premature deindustrialization · Future research

This book has surveyed the literature on automation and in doing so discussed definitions and determinants of automation in the context of theories of economic development, assessed the empirical estimates of employment-related impacts of automation and outlined the public policy responses to automation. We have shown that the contentious debate on automation is not new. Its origins can be traced back to classical political economy and thinking on economic development, and both the optimistic and pessimistic camps that have emerged over time have made valid points. To understand the employment dynamics of automation-driven structural change, the book used a simple framework in the tradition of W. Arthur Lewis (and William Baumol) and with recognition of Marx' reserve army thinking.

In conclusion, we would argue that the main implications of advances in technology and automation are not mass lay-offs and technological unemployment necessarily (though both are plausible under certain scenarios) in developing countries, but an increasing pressure toward deindustrialization and deagriculturalization. Empirically, the impact of automation is complex to estimate, and most studies have tended toward technologically deterministic approaches. Theoretically, the net effect on jobs could be both positive (lower prices lead to higher quantities demanded and thus more labor demand) and also negative (displaced labor is not absorbed in the ARS). Manual routine work, especially in agriculture, remains prevalent throughout the developing world, which is an important concern. Overall, the focus of many studies on employment is arguably too narrow, and there are broader questions about the impact of the digital revolution on structural change and strategies of economic development to be addressed.

The developing world could well experience more negative impacts from automation than the developed world, since (i) there are substantially more jobs to be lost through labor-substituting technical progress than in the rich world and (ii) new industries may stop outsourcing production to the developing world. We argue that it is likely that real wages may stagnate rather than unemployment rise per se in the developing world which implies sociopolitical consequences. This line of argument is, of course, particularly tailored to the characteristics of labor-abundant open economies and may not be generalizable beyond that.

One way or another, technological innovation is causing disruption and thus poses questions for public policy. We would express skepticism about the often-voiced call for skills-based development strategies alone.

Social safety nets, on the other hand, do seem to offer one strategy; yet, to the extent that they raise the cost of labor, could exacerbate the trend toward technological substitution. In this context, discussions about a living-wage level universal basic income (UBI) somewhat smack of a "first-world problem": to be able to worry about the redistribution of profits due to productivity gains assumes the luxury of jurisdiction over those profits, which many developing countries may not have. So, what to do?

We see the policy space for developing countries split between coping and containment strategies and constrained by globalization. Protectionist trade policy in the North could well accelerate reshoring, and hence the impacts on the developing world that this book discusses. In the long term, utopian as it may seem now, the moral case for a *global* UBI-style redistribution framework financed by profits from high-productivity production clusters in high-income countries may become overwhelming, but it is difficult to see how such a framework would be politically enacted. For the moment, in any case, workers in developing countries are facing an uphill battle against a growing "Robot Reserve Army".

Avenues for future research are numerous. Here we simply set out a range of indicative questions. The core research question is, given a context of automation and digitization, how are developing countries to increase the quantity and quality of employment growth? The core question can be broken down into three clusters of (indicative) subquestions. First, regarding the poverty–employment nexus: How/when/why does productivity growth translate into employment growth? What determines the distribution of productivity gains in terms of the functional distribution of income between capital and labor? Second, regarding the automation–employment nexus: Which tasks are being automated and by when? How do automation and digitization impact different developing countries, considering their specific production, employment, and export structures, and differing contexts? Third, regarding political and policy implications: What have been or are likely to be the political consequences of changes in employment due to automation and digitization? Under what conditions and circumstances can technological change and deindustrialization be inclusive? What factors incentivize and constrain the adoption of labor-saving technologies? And how have national and subnational governments responded to date? How have existing deindustrialization, automation, and its socioeconomic effects expressed themselves (or not) politically? What are the public policy options for governments? In sum, there are numerous questions arising for the future of economic development that automation throws up. Understanding the more precise impacts of automation on the economic development of developing countries can only be well understood if such questions are urgently pursued.

In conclusion, we would make three points. First, automation is challenging the competitive advantage of low-cost labor of late developers. Second, many developing countries have a vulnerable labor force in terms of wage stagnation and premature deindustrialization could loom. However, unemployment is not (yet) the problem. Third, we need to ask different policy and research questions and be concerned about the jobs impact of technology and the political economy of automation rather than just automatability in principle. In that vein the Lewis model and surplus labor theory could once more help us understand the dynamics of economic development and structural transformation.

Open Access This chapter is licensed under the terms of the Creative Commons Attribution 4.0 International License (http://creativecommons.org/licenses/by/4.0/), which permits use, sharing, adaptation, distribution and reproduction in any medium or format, as long as you give appropriate credit to the original author(s) and the source, provide a link to the Creative Commons license and indicate if changes were made.

The images or other third party material in this chapter are included in the chapter's Creative Commons license, unless indicated otherwise in a credit line to the material. If material is not included in the chapter's Creative Commons license and your intended use is not permitted by statutory regulation or exceeds the permitted use, you will need to obtain permission directly from the copyright holder.

Correction to: Disrupted Development and the Future of Inequality in the Age of Automation

Correction to:
L. Schlogl and A. Sumner, *Disrupted Development and the Future of Inequality in the Age of Automation*, Rethinking International Development series,
https://doi.org/10.1007/978-3-030-30131-6

The original version of this book was inadvertently published without the acknowledgement of the funder (Austrian Science Fund (FWF): PUB 676-Z). The book has been updated with the changes.

The updated version of the book can be found at
https://doi.org/10.1007/978-3-030-30131-6

© The Author(s) 2020
L. Schlogl and A. Sumner, *Disrupted Development and the Future of Inequality in the Age of Automation*, Rethinking International Development series, https://doi.org/10.1007/978-3-030-30131-6_8

REFERENCES

Acemoglu, D., & Autor, D. (2011). Skills, tasks and technologies: Implications for employment and earnings. In O. Ashenfelter & D. Card (Eds.), *Handbook of labor economics* (Vol. 4B, pp. 1043–1171). Amsterdam: Elsevier.

Acemoglu, D., & Restrepo, P. (2015). The race between machine and man: Implications of technology for growth, factor shares and employment. *SSRN Electronic Journal*. https://doi.org/10.2139/ssrn.2781320.

Acemoglu, D., & Restrepo, P. (2017). *Robots and jobs: Evidence from US labor markets* (NBER Working Paper Series No. 23285). Cambridge, MA: NBER. Retrieved from http://www.nber.org/papers/w23285.

Acemoglu, D., & Robinson, J. A. (2000). Political losers as a barrier to economic development. *American Economic Review Papers and Proceedings, 90*, 126–130.

ADB (Asian Development Bank). (2018). *Asian development outlook 2018: How technology affects jobs*. Manila: ADB.

Ahmed, M. (2017). Technological revolution and the future of work. *Center for global development blog*. Retrieved May 25, 2018, from https://www.cgdev.org/blog/technological-revolution-and-future-work.

Aisyah, R. (2017, November 3). No layoffs after full cashless payment: Toll road operator. *The Jakarta Post*. Retrieved from http://www.thejakartapost.com/news/2017/11/03/no-layoffs-after-full-cashless-payment-toll-road-operator.html.

Amirapu, A., & Subramanian, A. (2015). *Manufacturing or services? An Indian illustration of a development dilemma* (Center for Global Development Working Paper 409). Washington, DC: CGD.

Anand, R., Cheng, K. C., Rehman, S., & Zhang, L. (2014). *Potential growth in emerging Asia* (IMF Working Paper). Washington, DC: IMF.

Anderson, C. J. (2000). Economic voting and political context: A comparative perspective. *Electoral Studies, 19*(2–3), 151–170.

Arntz, M., Gregory, T., & Zierahn, U. (2016). The risk of automation for jobs in OECD countries: A comparative analysis. *OECD Social, Employment and Migration Working Papers, 2*(189), 47–54.

Atkinson, A. B. (2009). Factor shares: The principal problem of political economy. *Oxford Review of Economic Policy, 25*(1), 3–16.

Atkinson, A. B., & Bourguignon, F. (2014). Introduction: Income distribution today. In A. B. Atkinson & F. Bourguignon (Eds.), *Handbook of income distribution, volume 2A* (pp. xvii–lxiv). Oxford and Amsterdam: Elsevier.

Atkinson, R. D., & Wu, J. (2017). *False alarmism: Technological disruption and the U.S. labor market, 1850–2015.* @Work Series. Retrieved from http://www2.itif.org/2017-false-alarmism-technological-disruption.pdf.

Autor, D. H., & Dorn, D. (2013). The growth of low-skill service jobs and the polarization of the US labor market. *American Economic Review, 103*(5), 1553–1597.

Autor, D. H., Katz, L. F., & Kearney, M. S. (2004). The polarization of the U.S. labor market. *AEA Papers and Proceedings, 96*(2), 189–194.

Autor, D. H., Levy, F., & Murnane, R. J. (2003). The skill content of recent technological change: An empirical exploration. *The Quarterly Journal of Economics, 118*(4), 1279–1333.

Avent, R. (2017). *The wealth of humans: Work and its absence in the twenty-first century.* London: Penguin Random House.

Barany, Z., & Siegel, C. (2014). *Job polarization and structural change.* Retrieved from https://www.aeaweb.org/conference/2015/retrieve.php?pdfid=237.

Basu, D., & Foley, D. K. (2013). Dynamics of output and employment in the US economy. *Cambridge Journal of Economics, 37*(5), 1077–1106.

Baumol, W. J. (1967). Macroeconomics of unbalanced growth: The anatomy of urban crisis. *The American Economic Review, 57*(3), 415–426.

Baumol, W. J., Anne, S. U. E., Blackman, B., & Wolff, E. N. (1985). Unbalanced growth revisited: Asymptotic stagnancy and new evidence. *The American Economic Review, 75*(4), 806–817.

Berman, E., Bound, J., & Machin, S. (1998). Implications of skill-biased technological change: International evidence. *The Quarterly Journal of Economics, 113*(4), 1245–1279.

Bessen, J. (2016). *How computer automation affects occupations: Technology, jobs, and skills* (Law & Economics Working Paper No. 15–49). Boston, MA. Retrieved from https://papers.ssrn.com/sol3/papers.cfm?abstract_id=2690435.

Betcherman, G. (2012). *Labor market institutions: A review of the literature* (World Bank Policy Research Working Paper Series No. 6276). Washington, DC: World Bank.

Brynjolfsson, E., & McAfee, A. (2011). *Race against the machine: How the digital revolution is accelerating innovation, driving productivity, and irreversibly transforming employment and the economy.* Lexington, MA: Digital Frontier Press.

Brynjolfsson, E., & McAfee, A. (2014). *The second machine age: Work, progress, and prosperity in a time of brilliant technologies.* New York, NY and London: W. W. Norton.

Castells, M. (2010). *The rise of the network society: The information age: Economy, society, and culture.* Hoboken, NJ: Wiley Blackwell.

Chandy, L. (2017). *The future of work in the developing world: Brookings Blum roundtable 2016 post-conference report.* Washington, DC: Brookings Institution.

Chang, J.-H., & Huynh, P. (2016). *ASEAN in transformation: The future of jobs at risk of automation* (Bureau for Employers' Activities Working Paper No. 9). Bangkok. Retrieved from http://www.ilo.org/wcmsp5/groups/public/---ed_dialogue/---act_emp/documents/publication/wcms_579554.pdf.

Chenery, H. B. (1960). Patterns of industrial growth. *The American Economic Review, 50*(4), 624–654.

Chenery, H. B. (1975). The structuralist approach to development policy. *The American Economic Review, 65*(2), 310–316.

Chenery, H. B. (1979). *Structural change and development policy.* Washington, DC: World Bank and Oxford: Oxford University Press.

Christensen, C. (1997). *The innovator's dilemma: When new technologies cause great firms to fail.* Boston, MA: Harvard Business Review Press.

Clark, G. (2008). *A farewell to alms: A brief economic history of the world.* Princeton, NJ and Oxford: Princeton University Press.

Dasgupta, S., & Singh, A. (2006). *Manufacturing, services and premature deindustrialisation in developing countries: A Kaldorian analysis* (UNU-WIDER, United Nations University Research Paper, No. 2006/49). Helsinki: UNU-WIDER.

DeLong, B. (2015). *Technological progress anxiety: Thinking about "peak horse" and the possibility of "peak human".* Retrieved from http://equitablegrowth.org/equitablog/technological-progress-anxiety-thinking-about-peak-horse-and-the-possibility-of-peak-human/.

Deny, S. (2017, August 24). Sri mulyani khawatir generasi muda ri kalah dengan robot. *Liputan 6.* Retrieved from http://bisnis.liputan6.com/read/3069606/sri-mulyani-khawatir-generasi-muda-ri-kalah-dengan-robot.

Diao, X., McMillan, M., Rodrik, D., & Kennedy, J. F. (2017). *The recent growth boom in developing economies: A structural-change perspective* (NBER Working Paper Series No. 23132). Cambridge, MA: NBER. Retrieved from http://www.nber.org/papers/w23132.

Douglas, P. H. (1976). The Cobb-Douglas production function once again: Its history, its testing, and some empirical values. *Journal of Political Economy, 84*(5), 903–915.

Duarte, M., & Restuccia, D. (2010). The role of the structural transformation in aggregate productivity. *The Quarterly Journal of Economics, 125*(1), 129–173.

Eastwood, R., Kirsten, J., & Lipton, M. (2007). Premature deagriculturalisation? Land inequality and rural dependency in Limpopo province, South Africa. *The Journal of Development Studies, 42*(8), 1325–1349.

Executive Office of the President of the United States. (2016). *Preparing for the future of artificial intelligence*. Washington, DC. Retrieved from https://obamawhitehouse.archives.gov/sites/default/files/whitehouse_files/microsites/ostp/NSTC/preparing_for_the_future_of_ai.pdf.

Fei, J. C. H., & Ranis, G. (1964). *Development of the labor surplus economy: Theory and policy*. Homewood, IL: Richard A. Irwin.

Finseraas, H. (2009). Income inequality and demand for redistribution: A multilevel analysis of European public opinion. *Scandinavian Political Studies, 32*(1), 94–119.

Firpo, S. P., Fortin, N. M., & Lemieux, T. (2011). *Occupational tasks and changes in the wage structure* (IZA Discussion Paper No. 5542). Bonn: IZA. Retrieved from http://ftp.iza.org/dp5542.pdf.

Fischer, A. (2011). Beware the fallacy of productivity reductionism. *The European Journal of Development Research, 23*(4), 521–526.

Fischer, A. M. (2014). *The social value of employment and the redistributive imperative for development* (UNDP Human Development Report Office, Occasional Paper). New York: UNDP.

Francese, M., & Mulas-Granados, C. (2015). *Functional income distribution and its role in explaining inequality* (IMF Working Papers 15/244). Washington, DC: IMF. Retrieved from https://www.imf.org/en/Publications/WP/Issues/2016/12/31/Functional-Income-Distribution-and-Its-Role-in-Explaining-Inequality-43415.

Frey, C. B., & Osborne, M. A. (2013). *The future of employment: How susceptible are jobs to computerisation?* Oxford Martin School, University of Oxford Working Paper. University of Oxford, UK. Retrieved from https://www.oxfordmartin.ox.ac.uk/downloads/academic/future-of-employment.pdf.

Frey, C. B., Osborne, M. A., & Holmes, C. (2016). *Technology at work v2.0: The future is not what it used to be* (Citi GPS: Global Perspectives & Solutions). Oxford. Retrieved from http://www.oxfordmartin.ox.ac.uk/downloads/reports/Citi_GPS_Technology_Work_2.pdf.

Frey, C. B., & Rahbari, E. 2016. *Do labor-saving technologies spell the death of jobs in the developing world* (Paper prepared for the 2016 Brookings Blum Roundtable).

Goldin, C., & Katz, L. F. (2007). *The race between education and technology: The evolution of U.S. educational wage differentials, 1890 to 2005* (NBER Working Paper Series No. 12984). Cambridge, MA: NBER. Retrieved from http://www.nber.org/papers/w12984.

Gollin, D. M., Parente, S., and Rogerson, R. (2004). Farm Work, Home Work and International Productivity Differences. *Review of Economic Dynamics, 7*(4), 827–850.

Gollin, D. (2014). The Lewis model: A 60-year retrospective. *Journal of Economic Perspectives, 28*(3), 71–88.

Gollin, D., Jedwab, R., & Vollrath, D. (2016). Urbanization with and without structural transformation. *Journal of Economic Growth, 21*(1), 35–70.

Gomez, E., & Jomo, K. S. (1997). *Malaysia's political economy: Politics, patronage and profits*. Cambridge: Cambridge University Press.

Goos, M., & Manning, A. (2007). Lousy and lovely jobs: The rising polarization of work in Britain. *Review of Economics and Statistics, 89*(1), 118–133.

Grace, K., Salvatier, J., Dafoe, A., Zhang, B., & Evans, O. (2017). *When will AI exceed human performance? Evidence from AI experts* (arXiv No. 1705.08807v2). Retrieved from http://arxiv.org/abs/1705.08807.

Granstrand, O. (1994). *Economics of technology*. Amsterdam: North-Holland.

Hall, B. H., & Khan, B. (2003). *Adoption of new technology* (NBER Working Paper Series No. 9730). Cambridge, MA: NBER. Retrieved from http://www.nber.org/papers/w9730.

Hallward-Driemeier, M., & Nayyar, G. (2017). *Trouble in the making? The future of manufacturing-led development*. Washington, DC: World Bank.

Harari, Y. N. (2016). *Homo deus: A brief history of tomorrow*. London: Harvill Secker.

Harris, J. R., & Todaro, M. P. (1970). Migration, unemployment and development: A two-sector analysis. *American Economic Review, 60*, 126–142.

Heintz, J. (2009). *Employment, economic development and poverty reduction: Critical issues and policy challenges*. Geneva: UNRISD.

Herrendorf, B., Rogerson, R., & Valentinyi, A. (2014). *Growth and structural transformation* (NBER Working Paper Series No. 18996). Cambridge, MA: NBER. Retrieved from http://www.nber.org/papers/w18996.

Hirschman, A. O. (1958). *The strategy of economic development*. New Haven, CT: Yale University Press.

IFR. (2016). *Executive summary World robotics 2016 service robots* (International Federation of Robotics). Retrieved from http://www.ifr.org/fileadmin/user_upload/downloads/World_Robotics/2016/Executive_Summary_WR_Industrial_Robots_2016.pdf.

IGM Panel. (2014, February 25). Robots. *IGM Forum*. Retrieved from http://www.igmchicago.org/surveys/robots.

ILO. (2017). *The future of work we want: A global dialogue*. Geneva: International Labor Organization. Retrieved from http://www.ilo.org/global/topics/future-of-work/WCMS_570282/lang--en/index.htm.

IMF. (2017). *World economic outlook, April 2017: Gaining momentum?* Washington, DC: IMF. Retrieved from http://www.imf.org/en/Publications/WEO/Issues/2017/04/04/world-economic-outlook-april-2017.

Inglehart, R., & Welzel, C. (2005). *Modernization, cultural change, and democracy: The human development sequence*. Cambridge and New York, NY: Cambridge University Press.

Iversen, T., & Cusack, T. R. (2000). The causes of welfare state expansion: Deindustrialization or globalization. *World Politics, 52*(3), 313–349.

Jahoda, M., Lazarsfeld, P. F., & Zeisel, H. (1933). *Marienthal: The sociography of an unemployed community*. Leipzig: Hirzel Verlag.

Jakarta Globe. (2017, October 13). Indonesia to consider universal basic income. *Jakarta Globe*. Retrieved from http://jakartaglobe.id/business/indonesia-to-study-universal-basic-income/.

Jakarta Post. (2017, September 14). Non-cash toll will affect 10,000 workers in Jakarta. *The Jakarta Post*. Retrieved from http://www.thejakartapost.com/news/2017/09/14/non-cash-toll-will-affect-10000-workers-in-jakarta.html.

Jefriando, M. (2017, October 12). Sri mulyani bicara soal robot ancam pekerjaan manusia. *Detik*. Retrieved from https://finance.detik.com/berita-ekonomi-bisnis/3680492/sri-mulyani-bicara-soal-robot-ancam-pekerjaan-manusia.

Kaldor, N. (1957). A model of economic growth. *The Economic Journal, 67*(268), 591–624.

Kaldor, N. (1978 [1966]). *Causes of the slow rate of economic growth of the United Kingdom*. Cambridge: Cambridge University Press.

Kanbur, R. (2016). *W. Arthur Lewis and the Roots of Ghanaian Economic Policy* (Working Paper). Charles H. Dyson School of Applied Economics and Management Cornell University, Ithaca, New York.

Katz, L. F., & Autor, D. H. (1999). Changes in the wage structure and earnings inequality. In O. Ashenfeher & D. Card (Eds.), *Handbook of labor economics* (Vol. 3, pp. 1463–1555). Amsterdam: Elsevier.

Katz, L. F., & Murphy, K. M. (2013). Changes in relative wages, 1963–1987: Supply and demand factors. *The Quarterly Journal of Economics, 107*(1), 35–78.

Kuznets, S. (1971). *Modern economic growth: Findings and reflections: Lecture to the memory of Alfred Nobel*. Stockholm: The Nobel Foundation. Retrieved from http://www.nobelprize.org/nobel_prizes/economic-sciences/laureates/1971/kuznets-lecture.html.

Lacity, M., & Willcocks, L. P. (2018). *Robotic process and cognitive automation: The next phase*. Stratford: Steve Brookes Publishing.

Leontief, W., & Duchin, F. (1984). The impacts of automation on employment, 1963–2000. *CATESOL Journal, 5*(1), 1963–2000. Retrieved from http://files.eric.ed.gov/fulltext/ED241743.pdf.

Lewis, W. A. (1954). Economic development with unlimited supplies of labour. *The Manchester School of Economic and Social Studies, 22*(2), 139–191.

Lewis, W. A. (1979). The dual economy revisited. *The Manchester School, 47*(3), 211–229.

Lewis-Beck, M. S., & Stegmaier, M. (2000). Economic determinants of electoral outcomes. *Annual Review of Political Science, 3*, 183–219.

Marx, K. (2012 [1867]). *Das Kapital: A critique of political economy*. Washington, DC: Regnery Publishing.

McKinsey Global Institute. (2017a). *A future that works: Automation, employment, and productivity.* Retrieved from https://www.mckinsey.com/~/media/McKinsey/Global%20Themes/Digital%20Disruption/Harnessing%20automation%20for%20a%20future%20that%20works/MGI-A-future-that-works_Full-report.ashx.

McKinsey Global Institute. (2017b). *Jobs lost, jobs gained: Workforce transitions in a time of automation.* Retrieved from https://www.mckinsey.com/~/media/McKinsey/Global%20Themes/Future%20of%20Organizations/What%20the%20future%20of%20work%20will%20mean%20for%20jobs%20skills%20and%20wages/MGI-Jobs-Lost-Jobs-Gained-Report-December-6-2017.ashx.

McKinsey Global Institute. (2017c). *Where machines could replace humans—And where they can't (yet).* Retrieved from https://public.tableau.com/en-us/s/gallery/where-machines-could-replace-humans.

McMillan, M. S., & Rodrik, D. (2011). *Globalization, structural change and productivity growth* (NBER Working Paper Series No. 17143). Cambridge, MA: NBER. Retrieved from http://www.nber.org/papers/w17143.

Minami, R. (1973). *The turning point in economic development: Japan's experience.* Tokyo: Kinokuniya.

Mishel, L., & Bivens, J. (2017). *The zombie robot argument lurches on: There is no evidence that automation leads to joblessness or inequality.* Washington, DC: Economic Policy Institute. Retrieved from http://www.epi.org/files/pdf/126750.pdf.

Mokyr, J. (1998). The political economy of technological change: Resistance and innovation in economic history. In M. Berg & K. Bruland (Eds.), *Technological revolutions in Europe* (pp. 39–64). Cheltenham: Edward Elgar Publishers.

Mokyr, J., Vickers, C., & Ziebarth, N. L. (2015). The history of technological anxiety and the future of economic growth: Is this time different? *Journal of Economic Perspectives, 29*(3), 31–50.

Mughan, A. (2018). Economic insecurity and welfare preferences: A micro-level analysis. *Comparative Politics, 39*(3), 293–310. Retrieved from http://www.jstor.org/stable/20434042.

Myrdal, G. (1957a). *Rich lands and poor: The road to world prosperity.* New York: Harper & Brothers.

Myrdal, G. (1957b). *Economic theory and underdeveloped regions.* London: Gerald Duckworth & Co. Ltd.

Myrdal, G. (1968). *Asian drama: An inquiry into the poverty of nations.* New York: Pantheon Books.

Ngai, L. R., & Pissarides, C. A. (2017). Structural change in a multi-sector model of growth. *American Economic Review, 97*(1), 429–443.

Office for National Statistics. (2013). *170 years of industrial change across England and Wales.* Retrieved from http://webarchive.nationalarchives.gov.uk/20160106001413/http://www.ons.gov.uk/ons/rel/

census/2011-census-analysis/170-years-of-industry/170-years-of-industrial-changeponent.html.

Palma, J. G. (2005). Four sources of "de-industrialization" and a new concept of the "Dutch disease". In J. A. Ocampo (Ed.), *Beyond reforms: Structural dynamic and macroeconomic vulnerability* (pp. 71–116). Palo Alto, CA and Washington, DC: Stanford University Press and World Bank.

Parente, S. L., & Prescott, E. C. (1994). Barriers to technology adoption and development. *Journal of Political Economy, 102*(2), 298–321.

Pontusson, J., & Rueda, D. (2008). Inequality as a source of political polarization: A comparative analysis of twelve OECD countries. In P. Beramendi & C. Anderson (Eds.), *Democracy, inequality, and representation: A comparative perspective* (pp. 312–353). New York: Russell Sage Foundation.

Praditya, I. I. (2017, August 17). 72 tahun merdeka, ri masih hadapi deindustrialisasi. *Liputan 6.* Retrieved from http://bisnis.liputan6.com/read/3061377/72-tahun-merdeka-ri-masih-hadapi-deindustrialisasi.

PWC (PricewaterhouseCoopers). (2017). UK Economic Outlook.

Ranis, G. (2004). 'Arthur Lewis' contribution to development thinking and policy (Discussion Paper 891). Economic Growth Center Yale University.

Ricardo, D. (2010). *On the principles of political economy, and taxation.* Urbana, Illinois: Project Gutenberg. http://www.gutenberg.org/files/33310/33310-h/33310-h.htm.

Rodrik, D. (2016). Premature deindustrialization. *Journal of Economic Growth, 21*(1), 1–33.

Roine, J., & Waldenström, D. (2014). *Long-run trends in the distribution of income and wealth* (IZA Discussion Paper No. 8157). Bonn: IZA. Retrieved from http://ftp.iza.org/dp8157.pdf.

Rosenzweig, M. (1988). Labor markets in low income countries. In H. Chenery & T. N. Srinivasan (Eds.), *Handbook of development economics* (Vol. 1). Amsterdam: North Holland Press.

Rowthorn, R., & Ramaswamy, R. (1999). *Growth, trade, and deindustrialization* (IMF Staff Papers). Washington, DC: IMF.

Saragih, F. A. (2017, September 16). Otomatisasi tol dianggap kejahatan. *Kompas.com.* Retrieved from http://ekonomi.kompas.com/read/2017/09/16/080100530/otomatisasi-tol-dianggap-kejahatan.

Schumpeter, J. A. (1943). *Capitalism, socialism and democracy.* Abingdon-on-Thames: Routledge.

Schwab, K. (2016). *The fourth industrial revolution.* Geneva: Portfolio Penguin.

Siegel, D. S., Waldman, D. A., & Youngdahl, W. E. (1997). The adoption of advanced manufacturing technologies: Human resource management implications. *IEEE Transactions on Engineering Management, 44*(3), 288–298.

Solow, R. M. (1956). A contribution to the theory of economic growth. *The Quarterly Journal of Economics, 70*(1), 65–94.

Solow, R. M. (1964). *The nature and sources of unemployment in the United States*. Stockholm: Almqvist and Wicksell.
Srnicek, N. (2017). *Platform capitalism*. Cambridge and Malden, MA: Polity Press.
Storm, S. (2015). Structural change. *Development and Change, 46*, 666–699.
Summers, L. H. (2013). Economic possibilities for our children: The 2013 Martin Feldstein lecture. *NBER Reporter, 4*, 4–6. Retrieved from http://www.nber.org/reporter/2013number4/2013no4.pdf.
Sutirtha, R., Kessler, M., & Subramanian, A. (2016). *Glimpsing the end of economic history? Unconditional convergence and the missing middle-income trap* (Centre for Global Development Working Paper 438). Washington, DC: CGD.
Syrquin, M. (2007). *Kuznets and Pasinetti on the study of structural transformation: Never the Twain shall meet?* (International Centre for Economic Research Working Paper 46). Torino, Italy.
Targetti, F. (1988). *'Nicholas Kaldor', Teoria e politica economica di un capitalismo in mutamento*. Bologna: Società Editrice II Mulino S.p.A.
Targetti, F. (2005). Nicholas Kaldor: Key contributions to development economics. *Development and Change, 36*(6), 1185–1199.
Tempo. (2015, December 14). Provinsi di Indonesia ini alami gejala deindustrialisasi. *Tempo.co*. Retrieved from https://bisnis.tempo.co/read/727694/provinsi-di-indonesia-ini-alami-gejala-deindustrialisasi.
Tempo. (2016a, January 12). Bali bans the operation of Uber Taxi. *Tempo.co*. Retrieved from https://en.tempo.co/read/news/2016/01/21/056738210/Bali-Bans-the-Operation-of-Uber-Taxi.
Tempo. (2016b, March 21). Protes Uber dan Grab, sopir se-Jakarta akan unjuk rasa. *Tempo.co*. Retrieved from https://metro.tempo.co/read/755352/protes-uber-dan-grab-sopir-se-jakarta-akan-unjuk-rasa.
Tempo. (2016c, September 27) 200 Ribu pekerja terancam phk karena otomatisasi gardu tol. *Tempo.co*. Retrieved from https://bisnis.tempo.co/read/807738/200-ribu-pekerja-terancam-phk-karena-otomatisasi-gardu-tol.
Tempo. (2017, February 20). Era Digital, jumlah pengangguran meningkat. *Tempo.co*. Retrieved from https://tekno.tempo.co/read/848320/era-digital-jumlah-pengangguran-meningkat.
The Guardian. (2016, March 22). Traffic chaos and violence as thousands of taxi drivers protest against Uber in Jakarta. *The Guardian*. Retrieved from https://www.theguardian.com/world/2016/mar/22/traffic-chaos-and-violence-as-thousands-of-taxi-drivers-protest-uber-in-jakarta.
Thirlwall, A. P. (1979). The interaction between income and expenditure in the absorption approach to the balance of payments. *Journal of Macroeconomics, Elsevier, 1*(2), 237–240.
Thirlwall, A. P. (1982). Deindustrialisation in the UK. *Lloyd's Bank Review, 134*, 22–37.

Thirlwall, A. P. (2011). Balance of payments constrained growth models: History and overview. *PSL Quarterly Review, 64*(259), 307–351.

Timmer, M. P., de Vries, G. J., & de Vries, K. (2015). Patterns of structural change in developing countries. In J. Weiss & M. A. Tribe (Eds.), *Routledge handbook of industry and development* (pp. 65–83). London: Routledge.

Tinbergen, J. (1974). Substitution of graduate by other labour. *Kyklos, 27*(2), 217–226.

Tinbergen, J. (1975). Substitution of academically trained by other manpower. *Review of World Economics, 111*(3), 466–476.

Todaro, M. P. (1969). A model of labor migration and urban unemployment in less developed countries. *The American Economic Review, 59*, 138–148.

UNCTAD. (2017). *Trade and development report 2017—Beyond austerity: Towards a global new deal*. New York and Geneva: UNCTAD.

UNDP. (2015). *Work for human development: Human development report*. New York: UNDP.

UNIDO. (2016). *Industrial development report 2016: The role of technology and innovation in inclusive and sustainable industrial development*. Vienna: UNIDO.

Willcocks, Leslie P., & Lacity, Mary. (2016). *Service automation: Robots and the future of work*. Stratford: Steve Brookes Publishing.

Williams, R., & Edge, D. (1996). The social shaping of technology. *Research Policy, 25*(6), 865–899.

Wood, A. (2017). *Variation in structural change around the world, 1985–2015: Patterns, causes, and implications* (UNU-WIDER Working Paper). UNU-WIDER: Helsinki. Retrieved from https://www.wider.unu.edu/sites/default/files/wp2017-34.pdf.

World Bank. (2013). *World development report: Jobs*. Washington, DC: World Bank.

World Bank. (2016). *World development report: Digital dividends*. Washington, DC: World Bank.

World Bank. (2018). *World development indicators*. Retrieved from data.worldbank.org/data-catalog/world-development-indicators.

World Economic Forum. (2017a). *Impact of the fourth industrial revolution on supply chains*. Geneva: WEF.

World Economic Forum. (2017b). *The future of jobs and skills in the Middle East and North Africa: Preparing the region for the fourth industrial revolution* (Executive Briefing). Geneva: WEF.

Yan, A. (2017, June 12). Beijing's first driverless subway line starts test run. *CGTN*. Retrieved from https://news.cgtn.com/news/3d557a4d3249444e/share_p.html.

Yusuf, S. (2017). Automation, AI, and the emerging economies. *Center for Global Development Blog*. Retrieved May 25, 2018, from https://www.cgdev.org/publication/automation-ai-and-emerging-economies.

Index

A
Acemoglu, Daron, 2, 40, 43, 44, 54, 63
Africa, 22, 31, 64, 65, 67, 74
  Sub-saharan, 13, 28–31, 72
Agriculture, 3, 13, 15, 17, 18, 22, 24, 27–29, 31, 39, 52, 53, 57, 58, 67, 71, 72, 74, 86
Asia, 13, 22, 38, 64, 72, 74
  East, 14, 24, 25, 27–31
  South East, 38, 64
Automatability, 4, 56, 58, 62, 64–67, 69, 70, 72, 74, 88
  forecasts, 4, 61
Automation
  determinants of, 3, 4, 40, 86
  feasibility of, 40
  optimism, 62
  pessimism, 43, 44
  susceptibility, 2, 44, 64–66
Autor, David, 44, 54
Avent, Ryan, 2, 43, 59, 64

B
Baumol, W.J., 73, 86

C
Capital, 12–16, 22, 24, 25, 28, 30, 31, 40–44, 52, 53, 55, 57, 59–61, 63, 87
  accumulation, 13–16, 25, 28, 30, 31, 59, 60
  -labor complementarity, 15
Capitalism, 60
Classical theory, 80
Complementarity, 15, 41, 43, 53, 62, 73
Containment strategy, 87
Convergence, 12–14

D
Deagriculturalization, 86
Deindustrialization, 2, 3, 29, 71, 80, 86, 87
  premature, 2, 17, 25, 44, 58, 88

Developing countries, 2–4, 13, 16–18, 22, 25, 39, 40, 51, 52, 58, 61–64, 67, 71, 72, 74, 82, 86–88
Development theory, 3
Digitization, 2, 38, 39, 42, 43, 73, 87
Dilemma, 53, 58
Disrupted development, 52
Disruption, 42, 59, 63, 66, 73, 86
Distribution, 12, 44, 53, 57, 79, 87
  functional, 44, 57, 87
  income, 44, 57, 87
Dual Sector Model, 16, 17

E
Economic
  convergence, 12, 14
  development, 3, 4, 11–14, 16, 17, 21, 29, 39, 52, 54, 55, 57, 61, 66, 67, 71, 86, 88
  growth, 2, 12, 14, 17, 18, 22, 38, 42, 52
  inequality, 80
  output, 14
  redistribution, 82
Education, 51, 81, 82
Employment, 2, 4, 13, 15, 17, 18, 22–24, 26, 29–31, 39, 41, 44, 52, 53, 57–63, 65–72, 74, 79, 86, 87
Ethiopia, 14, 31, 64, 65
Exports, 13, 15, 16, 18, 22, 23, 27, 29, 30, 72

F
Factors of production, 12, 16, 22, 28–30
Frey, C.B., 2, 39, 62–64, 66
Future of work, 2

G
Groningen Growth and Development Centre (GGDC), 22
Gross Domestic Product (GDP), 14, 17, 18, 23, 24, 26, 29–31, 65
  Growth of the, 14

I
Income, 12, 14, 18, 26, 31, 44, 52, 53, 59, 63, 67, 70, 72, 74, 80, 82, 87
India, 26, 31, 64, 65
Indonesia, 31, 41, 72
Industrialization, 14, 15
Inequality, 3, 14, 44, 53, 54, 63
Infrastructure, 82
Innovation, 39, 42, 52, 57, 73, 80, 86

J
Job, 2, 3, 40, 41, 43, 44, 55, 58, 59, 61–64, 72, 74, 81, 86, 88
  polarization, 44

K
Kaldor, Nicholas, 12, 14–16, 18, 26, 31
Kenya, 31, 38, 64
Korea, 38, 65
Kuznets, Simon, 42, 53, 72

L
Labor
  demand, 15, 16
  displacement, 39, 74
  exchange, 13, 55, 60
  force, 2, 18, 29, 31, 43, 52, 57, 59, 61, 66, 67, 72, 81, 88
  human, 28, 31, 43, 52, 57, 58

substitution, 87
supply, 15, 16, 57
surplus, 13, 16–18
Lewis, W.Arthur, 12–17, 31, 54, 55, 57, 59–61, 73, 74, 86, 88

M

Machinery, 38, 42, 59
Malthusianism, 60
Manufacturing, 12–15, 18, 23–30, 38, 52, 58, 63, 73, 74, 82
Market, 12, 13, 15–18, 42–44, 54, 55, 63, 66, 67, 73, 79–81
Marx, Karl, 38, 59–61, 73, 80, 86
McKinsey Global Institute, 2, 40, 41, 64–67, 70, 74
Mokyr, Joel, 2, 42, 80

N

Neoclassical theory, 12
Neo-Schumpeterianism, 11, 12

O

Occupation, 3, 63, 64, 73
Organisation for Economic Co-operation and Development (OECD), 2, 38, 43, 51, 62–55, 72, 73
Osborne, M.A., 2, 39, 62, 63
Outsourcing, 18, 86

P

Politics, 80
Poverty, 2, 3
  reduction, 3
Premature deindustrialization, 2, 17, 25, 44, 58, 88

Production, 12, 17, 24, 31, 38–40, 42–44, 52–54, 57, 59, 60, 80, 82, 86, 87
Productivity, 4, 12–18, 22, 23, 26, 28, 30, 31, 38, 41, 43, 44, 52–55, 58, 60, 61, 72–74, 87
  growth, 4, 14, 15, 17, 28, 44, 87
Profits, 16, 31, 53, 55, 82, 87
Public policy, 3, 4, 80, 81, 86, 88

R

Redistribution, 82, 87
Regulation, 4, 40, 80, 81
Reserve army, 59–61, 86
  industrial, 59
  of the Unemployed, 60
  robot, 57, 87
Reshoring, 52, 59, 82, 87
Robots, 37–39, 42, 43, 52, 53, 57, 73
Rodrik, Dani, 2, 13, 17, 18, 54, 55, 72

S

Schumpeter, J.A., 38, 42
Sector
  agricultural, 15, 52, 58
  automation-prone, 55
  automation-resistant, 57
  industrial, 15, 57, 58
  service, 13, 25, 52, 58, 67
  subsistence, 16, 17, 55, 57, 73
  traditional, 16, 54, 55, 57
  urban, 17, 60
Services, 13, 15, 17, 18, 24–27, 30, 39, 52, 58, 64, 67, 73, 82
Skills, 16, 43, 61, 62, 72, 81
Social, 3, 4, 31, 40, 42, 44, 58, 59, 80, 82, 87
  protection, 80
Solow, R.M., 12, 15, 42, 52–54

Structural, 12–14, 16–18, 21, 23, 39, 54–57, 59, 61, 62, 67, 71–73, 81, 86, 88
  change, 13, 54, 56, 57, 59, 61, 62, 67, 71–73, 81, 86
  transformation, 12–14, 16, 18, 21, 23, 39, 72, 88
Subsidies, 73, 81
Surplus labor, 55, 57, 58, 60, 61, 72, 88

T

Tasks, 39–41, 43, 44, 55, 57, 62–64, 67, 81, 87
Technological, 2, 3, 12, 14, 15, 18, 37–40, 42, 52–54, 57, 58, 60–63, 72, 80, 86, 87
  change, 12, 38, 42, 52–54, 58, 80, 87
  transformation, 39
  unemployment, 3, 39, 44, 53, 57, 86
Technology, 3, 4, 12, 13, 40, 42–44, 52–54, 60, 62, 64, 66, 72, 81, 86, 88
Tertiarization, 3
Thailand, 31, 65, 72
Tinbergen, Jan, 43, 54, 72
Trade, 18, 22, 28–30, 39, 73, 87

Transformation, 12–14, 16, 18, 21, 23, 38, 39, 54, 59, 60, 71–73, 88
  structural, 12–14, 16, 18, 21, 23, 39, 71, 72, 88
  technological, 39

U

Unemployment, 16, 18, 30, 44, 54, 55, 60, 67, 81, 86, 88
  disguised, 16, 30, 55, 60
  technological, 3, 39, 44, 53, 57, 86
Universal Basic Income (UBI), 41, 44, 81, 87
  global, 87

W

Wage, 3, 4, 14–17, 30, 43, 44, 53, 55, 57, 59–64, 72, 73, 79–81, 86–88
Work, 4, 14, 42–44, 57, 58, 61, 62, 64, 67, 71, 72, 80, 81, 86
  future of, 2
  manual, 43
  routine, 62, 86
World Bank, 2, 41, 64–68, 70, 71

The manufacturer's authorised representative in the EU is Springer Nature Customer Service Centre GmbH, Europaplatz 3, 69115 Heidelberg, Germany. If you have any concerns regarding our products, please contact ProductSafety@springernature.com

Printed and bound by CPI Group (UK) Ltd, Croydon, CR0 4YY

23/03/2026

02076449-0005